Time of Transitions

Jürgen Habermas

Edited and translated
by Ciaran Cronin and Max Pensky

polity

First published in German as *Zeit der Übergänge* and
© Suhrkamp Verlag Frankfurt am Main, 2001.

This English translation is © Polity, 2006.

Chapter 12 first appeared in "Religion and Rationality: Essays on
Reason, God, and Modernity," by Jürgen Habermas and edited by
Eduardo Mendieta, English translation © Polity Press, 2002.

The right of Jürgen Habermas to be identified as Author of this
Work has been asserted in accordance with the UK Copyright,
Designs and Patents Act 1988.

First published by Polity in 2006.

Polity Press
65 Bridge Street
Cambridge CB2 1UR, UK.

Polity Press
350 Main Street
Malden, MA 02148, USA

ISBN: 0-7456-3010-3
ISBN: 0-7456-3011-1 (pb)

A catalogue record for this book is available from the British
Library.

Typeset in 10.5 on 12 pt Berling
by SNP Best-set Typesetter Ltd, Hong Kong
Printed and bound in India by Replika Press

For further information on Polity, visit our website:
www.polity.co.uk

Contents

Editors' Preface   vii
Author's Foreword   xv

Part I From Bonn to Berlin   1

1   There are Alternatives!   3

Part II Interventions   17

2   From Power Politics to Cosmopolitan Society   19
3   A Sort of Logo of the Free West   31
4   The Finger of Blame: The Germans and
    Their Memorial   38

Part III Public Representation and Cultural Memory   51

5   Symbolic Expression and Ritual Behavior:
    Ernst Cassirer and Arnold Gehlen Revisited   53

Part IV Europe in Transition   71

6   Euroskepticism, Market Europe, or a Europe of
    (World) Citizens?   73
7   Does Europe Need a Constitution?   89

Part V A Question of Political Theory   111

8   Constitutional Democracy – A Paradoxical Union
    of Contradictory Principles?   113

Part VI American Pragmatism and German Philosophy:
Three Reviews   129

  9 John Dewey, *The Quest for Certainty*   131
10 Richard Rorty, *Achieving our Country*   136
11 Robert Brandom, *Making it Explicit*   142

Part VII Jerusalem, Athens, and Rome   147

12 A Conversation about God and the World   149

Notes   170
Index   182

Editors' Preface

Time of Transitions, which bears the subtitle "Short Political Writings IX" in the German, is the ninth in a series of volumes devoted to the author's essays and interviews on current political events stretching back to the 1960s. This testifies to the remarkable span of time during which the German-reading public could count on one thing: no matter how tempestuous and unpredictable the course of German politics, no matter how deep or frequent the debate, controversy, or crisis, an essay by Jürgen Habermas would address it with a distinctive combination of analytical insight and political passion. For more than 40 years, from the earliest efforts at rebuilding a democratic culture out of the rubble of totalitarianism, through Germany's struggle with its identity as it re-emerged as a major economic and political power, to the politics of unification and the united Germany's role as an influential global political actor, Habermas's status as an indispensable voice in the German public sphere has remained one of the rare constants.

The present volume differs from other recent collections of his political writings, such as *The Inclusion of the Other* or *The Postnational Constellation*, in blending essays and interviews on contemporary German politics and society with more wide-ranging studies. An important source of thematic unity is, as the title implies, a concern with processes of transition that have shaped or are currently shaping the course of European and world history. The transition which provides the context for all of the others discussed is the process of social modernization which has penetrated and transformed every aspect of life in Western societies while extending inexorably to ever-further reaches of the globe. Habermas's social and political thought has been devoted to the theoretical understanding of this process and to the articulation of its rational moments on which more just and humane conditions of social life could be founded. In this, he has shown particular sensitivity to the pathologies of modernization, its capacity to destroy the cultural resources necessary for a human existence worthy of the name, and its extraordinary potential for violence, injustice, and inhumanity as witnessed by the history of the twentieth century.

A more restricted historical context for the essays is provided by the process of globalization and the resulting need for a transition from the classical international order of sovereign nation-states to a transnational political order, which Habermas argues should take the form of a "global domestic politics without a world government." A still more narrowly circumscribed context is the transition toward greater political integration within an expanding European Union, a process wth important implications for political developments at the global level. And, finally, there are the longer- and shorter-term transitions of the Federal Republic of Germany which have been the focus of some of Habermas's most impassioned political interventions: the still incomplete postwar transition from the barbarity of the Nazi period to a functioning constitutional democracy, a learning process marked by denials and regressions, but also by notable, if painfully won, achievements; the post-1989 transition from a divided to a "reunited" Germany and the challenge of forging a democratic collective identity under the ambivalent aegis of a "Berlin Republic"; and the transition just begun from a necessarily restrictive understanding of Germany's role in European and world politics to the more expansive role demanded by its economic strength, its importance for European political integration, and its proximity to actual and potential crisis zones in Eastern Europe.

A major question posed by all of these transitions for Habermas is the extent to which the autonomous political practice of democratic citizens, rather than the logic of supposedly "impersonal" economic forces, will determine the course they take. The urgency of the associated challenges can be seen from the fact that, unless modes of democratic political organization and legitimation emerge above the level of nation-states, market-driven globalization threatens to undermine social solidarity within constitutional democracies and to aggravate global injustice and insecurity, not to mention environmental destruction and climate change.

The immediate occasion for the interview which opens the collection was a transition within the transition from Bonn to the Berlin Republic, namely, the 1998 election victory of the "Red-Green" coalition of the Social Democrats and the Greens under Gerhard Schröder and Joschka Fischer, following 16 years of center-right governments under Helmut Kohl. Habermas does not disguise his dismay at the climate of political, economic, and cultural stagnation which gripped the country as the euphoria of the reunification process subsided and which he (rightly!) feared the new government would do little to alter. A major cause of the malaise, he thinks, is the failure to grasp the global dimension of the political challenges facing the country – most ominously, mass unemployment – and the illusion that effective social and economic reforms can still be undertaken at the national level. Yet he refuses to accept that there are no alternatives to a supine politics that merely reacts to the pressures of globalizing markets and thereby consents to its own increasing irrelevance. The alternative he proposes is a politics that responds in a self-critical, reflexive fashion to the growing restrictions on the room for maneuver of the nation-state. This would involve cooperating in the construction of transnational and supranational political institutions and fostering the cultural resources for a transnational public sphere through which the decisions and policies of these institutions could acquire democratic legitimacy. On this analysis, the challenge is to continue the project of constitutional democracy beyond the nation-state with the goal of securing the fragile bases of social solidarity painfully won by the welfare state and promoting democracy and social justice in other regions of the world.

In addition to his advocacy of a "postnational" renewal of the project of constitutional democracy, Habermas here strikes a number of chords that resonate throughout the collection. For example, his suspicion of Schröder's attempts to disguise the poverty of genuine political initiatives through a cultural politics of national symbols, for which the move of the capital from Bonn to Berlin provided ample opportunity, reflects an awareness of the enduring importance of public symbols for forging a collective identity and a shared political culture in constitutional democracies. This is all the more true in the case of Germany, where the public representation and interpretation of symbols of national identity, and especially those associated with the former "imperial capital" Berlin, is inextricably bound up with the process of coming to terms with the Nazi past.

The three short polemical "Interventions" which make up the second part of the volume address three crucial issues in the current German political landscape. The 1999 NATO attacks on Yugoslavia to halt the Kosovo crisis provoked widespread debates in Germany concerning the role that the recently reunified nation should play in military interventions beyond its borders and the political future of regional and global institutions such as NATO and the United Nations. For a nation that had constructed its special form of "normality" on a postwar renunciation of militarism, calls to join a NATO interventionary force in Kosovo that lacked authorization from the UN Security Council were especially wrenching. Among other things, they signaled that Germany would be increasingly forced to confront its altered status in the international community as well as demands to assume greater political responsibilities at the regional and global levels. Viewed within the context of the transition to a postnational political order, the intervention revealed the pitfalls of a politics of human rights and humanitarian intervention, however urgent and compelling its moral motives, that lacks adequate supranational legal and institutional support, and hence the need to work toward the kind of postnational global constitutional order advocated by Habermas.

Around the same time, the so-called "political donations scandal" was rocking Germany, with daily revelations of an extraordinary history of corruption within the conservative Christian Democratic Union (CDU), the party of Helmut Kohl and the senior partner in the coalition governments led by Kohl from 1982 to 1998. A political culture that was no stranger to scandals was finding it difficult to acknowledge the nature of the scandal, and in particular the scale of the corruption it revealed among some of its highest elected officials. In the essay, "A Sort of Logo of the Free West," Habermas argues that what set the affair apart was precisely that it was *not* a matter of "politics as usual." Behind the anomalies of the scandal – in particular, the obtuse behavior of the principal figures and their stubborn refusal to follow the customary media "script" of such scandals – lurked the fact that the political leadership of a major national party had over decades adopted a purely instrumental attitude toward the federal constitution, which, for Habermas, represents the indispensable basis of Germany's "constitutional patriotism." For this reason, the depth of the scandal is matched by the depth of Habermas's anger. (Also there is some small irony in the fact that the conciliatory tone of Habermas's leave-taking from Kohl in the opening interview was soon to be so rudely disturbed as Kohl once again cast his considerable shadow across German postwar history!)

The third of these brief interventions, "The Finger of Blame," deals with perhaps the most insistent leitmotif in the history of the Federal Republic and a major preoccupation of Habermas's moral and political thought, the challenge of coming to terms with the National Socialist past. The project to erect a "Memorial to the Murdered Jews of Europe," a field of massive concrete stelae designed by the American architect Peter Eisenmann, in the heart of Berlin provoked heated debates throughout its protracted history. Inevitably, debates over the design, layout, and features of the planned memorial touched off deeper "ethical-political" debates concerning the meaning and function of historical memory in the constitution of German political identity. Always wary of voices which seek to declare an end to the process of coming to terms with the Nazi past in the name of a recovered "normality," Habermas defends a strikingly austere interpretation of the meaning of the memorial whose complex motivations leave it open to misunderstanding. The authors of the memorial are the German descendants of the perpetrators, he argues, and only they, and not the descendants of the victims, be they German Jews or Sinti or Roma, can determine what the memorial should mean. Although the commemoration of the Holocaust must not be instrumentalized for the purposes of forging a collective political identity, nevertheless, what is at stake is the critical appropriation of history as a necessary precondition for Germans' exercise of political autonomy in the present and in the future.

Some valuable light is thrown on the ideas informing Habermas's position on the memorial by the essay on "Symbolic Expression and Ritual Behavior," which forms the third part of the book. Through an interpretation of the contrasting theories of institutions and symbolization of the philosopher Ernst Cassirer and the philosophical anthropologist Arnold Gehlen, Habermas shows how subtle differences in their respective understandings of humans as symbolizing animals, and the role that this capacity plays in the development of social institutions, acquire enhanced significance when refracted through the prism of German political culture. On Habermas's account, Cassirer's and Gehlen's positions represent two stages in the divided philosophical and political reception of Hegel's theory of the individual and the state. But whereas Cassirer remained to the end committed to an Enlightenment conception of social and political institutions as enabling autonomous, symbolically self-constituting subjects to realize their freedom, the "young conservative" Gehlen understood symbolization as a compensatory faculty of a congenitally unadapted, hence weak and vulnerable, organism, which requires strong institutions to protect it from the forces of internal and external nature that threaten to overwhelm it.

The two essays on "Europe in Transition," which make up the fourth part of the book, constitute a major restatement and clarification of a thesis that Habermas has defended since the early 1990s, namely, that the European Union represents an important contemporary experiment in postnational democratic governance. What course this experiment will take – in particular, what form the transition to a closer political union in Europe will take – depends largely on the unresolved question of whether the EU continues to understand itself as an economic consortium vying for market share with other global economic players, or whether the process of European political integration develops into a political experiment of genuinely global significance. If the latter is to transpire, the EU will have to assume the form of a postnational democratic polity capable of responding to the challenges of globalization not just at the economic level but also in the dimensions of security, communications, the environment, migration, and culture, among others. In these essays, Habermas addresses two important preconditions for the success of this European political project: first, democratic politics, which has until now been conducted exclusively within the confines of nation-states, will have to undergo a self-reflexive transformation with the goal of enhancing political agencies above the level of the nation-state; second, if the legislative decisions and policies of supranational political agencies are to acquire democratic legitimacy – in particular, if the current "democratic deficit" of the EU institutions is to be overcome – new transnational forms of democratic political culture will have to develop based on a complex intermeshing of the public spheres of the member states.

The "Question of Political Theory" addressed in the fifth part of the collection is: how should we understand the relation between democracy and its defining principle of "popular sovereignty," on the one hand, and the constitutional basic rights which secure the "rule of law" on which the individual liberties of liberal democracies are founded, on the other? The insight informing Habermas's mature legal and political theory is that these principles are "co-original," that is, that popular sovereignty and the rule of law mutually imply each other;

hence, the legal and political institutions of constitutional democracies must be designed in such a way that they simultaneously promote individual liberty and the democratic legitimacy of law and political power. A key assumption of Habermas's approach is that human rights should be understood primarily as legal rights and, as such, must be implemented in positive law. In the present essay, he responds to a series of criticisms of his discursive model of democratic legitimation by the American constitutional theorist, Frank Michelman. Michelman's chief criticism is that Habermas cannot explain how a democratic constitution could be founded in the first place because the founding process cannot, on pain of circularity or regress, itself be procedurally legitimated, as Habermas's model requires; for the founding must first establish the necessary legal preconditions for all further democratic legitimation procedures. Habermas's response represents an important development of his procedural model of democratic legitimation: once we understand a democratic constitution as a project – specifically, as a collective learning process that unfolds over time in the medium of democratic discourse – then it becomes apparent that the founding act which gave rise to this project can acquire legitimacy *retrospectively* over time.

The three short book reviews which constitute the sixth part of the collection provide valuable insights into the influence of American pragmatism on Habermas's thought and his understanding of its significance for postwar German philosophy. Most striking is the emphasis he places on the Hegelian roots of pragmatism. The Hegelian legacy ensures a fertile ground for the belated German reception of a classic work such as Dewey's *Quest for Certainty* and for the current vogue of a major contemporary work such as Brandom's *Making it Explicit*, at a time when the American philosophical mainstream remains hostile both to the speculative ambitions of German idealism and to the primacy of the practical at the root of American pragmatism. Most germane to the political concerns of the present volume, however, is the review of Rorty's *Achieving our Country*. For it shows how Rorty, through a patriotic critique of the political paralysis of the American "new Left," converges on positions similar to those at which Habermas arrives through a critique of currents within German public life which seek to exploit national symbols to foster a false sense of normality.

The book concludes with a wide-ranging interview on the role of religion and religious attitudes in the "postmetaphysical" modern world. Here Habermas addresses a still more ancient transition, that from the archaic world of mythic powers and social structures founded on kinship to monotheistic religion, rational speculation and republican self-determination – symbolized by the names "Jerusalem, Athens, and Rome" – which created the necessary preconditions for the later transition from traditional to modern societies. His remarks on the relation between religion and philosophy, on religious conflict and toleration, on fundamentalism and the appeal to Christian solidarity in the face of global injustice and human suffering, reflect his conviction that, with the transition to a postmetaphysical world, religious claims to truth and validity must become self-reflexive in ways that enable them to acknowledge the rival claims of other religious traditions, as well as the competing truths of science and secular morality. Readers who are familiar with Habermas's works in social and political theory, in which religion figures more at the margins than the center, may be surprised to discover what an important role religious ideas, and ideas about religion, play in his understanding of his thought and its development. However, he is equally insistent that a strict methodological separation must be maintained between philosophy, on the one hand, and religion and theology, on the other. For, with the irreversible differentiation of reason into distinct domains and functions under conditions of modernity, contemporary philosophy would ignore this separation at the cost of forfeiting its claim to seriousness.

Note on the Translation

We have drawn freely on the following existing translations of individual chapters and hereby express our gratitude to the translators and publishers concerned: "Bestiality and Humanity: A War on the Border between Law and Morality" (chapter 2), trans. Franz Solms-Laubach (www.theglobalsite.ac.uk); "The European Nation-State and the Pressures of Globalization" (chapter 6), trans. G. M. Goshgarian (*New Left Review*, 1999, 235:46–59); "Why Europe Needs a Constitution" (chapter 7), (*New Left Review*, new series, 2001, 11:5–26). We are particularly indebted to William Rehg for permission to reprint his translation of chapter 8 (*Political Theory*, 2001, 29/6: 766–781) and for helpful comments on an earlier draft of the preface.

Author's Foreword

The Peace Prize of the German Book Trade is not intended to honor an academic work but to recognize an intellectual role. This encourages me to continue a series of "short political writings" stretching from *Protest Movements and University Reform* (1969), through *The New Obscurity* (1985), to *The Normality of a Berlin Republic* (1995). To be sure, the Red-Green government is still in transition to a Berlin Republic and its loudly trumpeted normality. A change in mentality can't be simply launched. The European Union is also still engaged in a process of transition toward an enlarged and consolidated political shape that remains elusive. Equally unsettling are the risks of the transition from classical international law to a cosmopolitan society; for we are still very far removed from the goal of a global domestic politics without a world government.

The stalled economic recovery seems to lend its signature to a period of stalled transitions in general.

The lectures, interviews, and reviews collected here date from the last three years.

Jürgen Habermas
Starnberg, June 2001

Part I

From Bonn to Berlin

The following interview with Gunter Hofmann and Thomas Assheuer on the "Prospects for the Red-Green Coalition" (which appeared in *Die Zeit*, October 8, 1998) took place immediately following the German federal elections.

1

There are Alternatives!

Question: Herr Habermas, for the first time in the history of the Federal Republic a sitting Chancellor has been voted out of office. Can we draw any conclusions from this about the state of democracy in Germany?

J. H.: I think so. Until now, changes in the ruling coalition were made by tactical agreements among political parties before the end of the scheduled parliamentary term. This is what led to the resignations of both Ludwig Erhart and Helmut Schmidt. This time, citizens took the lead in voting a sitting Chancellor out of office. In a democracy, the citizens need to be convinced that at decisive turning-points their votes really can influence hermetic political processes. In the "old" Federal Republic, it took several decades for a democratic sensibility like this to take root. I have a sense that this process is now more or less complete.

Question: For you, Helmut Kohl always represented a guarantor of the Federal Republic's orientation to the West. Will you miss him?

J. H.: All the criticisms have already been made. Kohl's historical achievement was to link the reunification of Germany with the unification of Europe. But my generation also recognizes him as one of our own. I'm thinking of his almost physical repudiation of the kind of "aesthetics of the state" demanded by our intellectual elites, especially since 1989. Clearly, Kohl never forgot the grotesque orchestration of the "Reich Party Days" and the Chaplinesque Nazi officials.

Of course, we often groaned over his provincialism and the clumsiness of his gestures and speech. Still, his deflation of empty claims and trivialization of public representation made him into a sympathetic figure for me. This also involved a degree of oppositional mentality that my generation embraced, if that is not too presumptuous. Perhaps we thereby succeeded in making some inroads against German intellectual pretentiousness, with its inflated interiority, abject pomposity, and compulsive sublimity. What's more, Kohl actually accomplished something in spite of himself. The failure of his "moral-intellectual turn" functioned as a litmus test.[1] The fact that Kohl could no longer do as he pleased once in government, at Verdun, Bitburg, and elsewhere, showed that the country had become liberal. A mental constant in the early years of the Federal Republic was the old Schmittian suspicion of "internal enemies" on the Left. This deep-seated anxiety of subversives broke out again in the pogrom mood of fall 1977.[2] Kohl could no longer feed off this sentiment.

Question: So now we're going to have a Red-Green government. Is this merely a political change? Or does it also mark a cultural shift?

J. H.: When the unprecedented magnitude of the Left's margin of victory became clear on the evening of the election, many of us older people were reminded of a day in the spring of 1969. Following his election as president of the Federal Republic, Heinemann had spoken of a "small change in power."[3] And shortly afterwards Willy Brandt completed the change with a wafer-thin majority for the socialist-liberal coalition. At that time, the long-delayed end of the Adenauer era was convincingly embodied by the upright figure of his adversary Heinemann. I experienced the foregoing years as a period that was politically and morally poisoned by fatal personal and mental continuities with the Nazi period. However, that rupture had been prepared by a decade of dogged intellectual opposition and then a further decade of active confrontation. On that occasion, politics merely recapitulated the shift in the cultural climate. The current situation does not bear comparison. For years nothing has managed to change the diffuse and crippling cultural climate here in Germany, and certainly not the nostrums of the alliance between smug neoliberalism and jaded postmodernism. After all, the excitement over yesterday's landslide victory is already almost completely forgotten.

Question: Can there really be a Red-Green project? Or does the limited room for political maneuver mean that only "variants of centrism" are possible?

J. H.: Until the end of the 1980s, there was a Red-Green project as long as a victory by Oskar Lafontaine in the next federal election seemed likely.[4] Under the pressure of the realities of German unification and a globalized economy, the project was whittled down to the slogan "Modernization and Social Justice" – salved with a dollop of eco-tax reform, if only to secure the necessary financing. It's not so much the disillusioned pragmatism that bothers me. The entire perspective was based on a false premise, namely, that the goals of social and economic reform could be realized within a national framework. In the meantime, a largely defensive politics has had to adapt to a transformed, postnational constellation. What bothers me is the lack of any new perspective. Today everybody is talking about the "post-ideological" era. But over the past 50 years, since Daniel Bell's *The End of Ideology*, this slogan has been invoked far too often and subsequently disclaimed to be at all plausible. In politics nothing changes without a divisive issue. And that's what's missing.

Question: Experience with older projects saps people's enthusiasm for new ones. What do you mean by a "project"?

J. H.: A "project" can only mean that you have a controversial issue and offer an analysis that defines the perceived problems more clearly and renders some political goals more plausible than others. That was missing in the election campaign. At any rate, the challenger studiously avoided any polarizing or controversial issue. And already on the evening of the election you could tell from the losers' relaxed expressions that their talk of a "change in direction" was not really serious.

Question: Which means that there are no alternatives?

J. H.: On the contrary. The most urgent problem for the new government is staring us straight in the face: what can be done about mass unemployment? Yet the room for maneuver of national governments has shrunk in two crucial ways. First, the effective ability of the state to tap the tax resources of the domestic economy is decreasing. And second, in an economy less and less contained within national borders, the familiar macroeconomic steering mechanisms are increasingly prone to failure. Hence the question of how politics and the economy are related is today being posed in a new, more reflexive form. Politicians must ask themselves whether they should continue with a politics of deregulation that will end up by making them redundant. Oversimplifying somewhat, does the loss of efficacy of politics at the national level imply the abdication of politics altogether, or can the political medium regenerate itself at other levels and make up the ground lost to transnational markets? This raises the issue of whether there can and should be a democratically legitimate exercise of power beyond the level of the nation-state. New political objectives would then follow from the regulatory needs arising at our doorstep, now that monetary union has set the seal on the European single market.

Question: In your new book, *The Postnational Constellation*, you argued that politicians should finally overcome their deep-seated inhibitions and reconstruct the welfare state at the supranational level. Is this the challenge against which the success of Gerhard Schröder's policies should be measured?

J. H.: That's precisely my view. I am indeed looking beyond Europe toward a global domestic politics without a world government. But first we must decide whether we really want to construct a Europe with genuine political powers. Waigel's slogan, "The Euro speaks German," is merely an oath of allegiance to a non-political institution, the European Central Bank.[5] Gerhard Schröder knows that the introduction of the Euro has made the problem of tax harmonization more acute. He explained this following the election using the example of the price of petrol. My sense is that we have to work toward an inner-European agreement on social and economic policy if we are to avoid a race to the bottom between the various systems of social policy of the member states. On the other hand, neo-corporatist measures have their limits. Effective redistribution policies can't be simply proclaimed in Brussels; they require democratic legitimation. Does this mean that we need a politically empowered European federal state if we want to avoid a further increase in social inequality and the emergence and segmentation of a mass of poor people? That's a controversial question. We're already witnessing a reversal of old alliances. Market Europeans who are happy with the Euro are now joining forces with former Euro-skeptics and insisting on the *status quo* of a Europe that is united solely by the creation of markets.

Question: Given that scarcely any supranational institutions exist at present, wouldn't it make more sense to exploit national capacities first before taking leave of the nation-state?

J. H.: The nation-state will remain the single most important political actor for the foreseeable future. It can't be dismissed so easily. Moreover, I think it's good that we now have a government that can be counted on to undertake every serious reform, beginning at the national level. I don't doubt that the "hard slog" which Schröder now wants to undertake in implementing his clever reform proposals and tried and trusted recipes may have some success. But this in no way alters the new dependency of the state on fundamentally altered global economic conditions. The question is whether the postnational constellation also calls for other political agencies with greater scope for action.

Question: Isn't society more intelligent and aware of its problems than we give it credit for? Even the experts at the Deutsche Bank want to domesticate capitalism.

J. H.: I don't know what is going on in the experts' heads. I can only observe how economic, political and scientific managers act – for example, when they negotiate the Multilateral Agreement on Investment now awaiting ratification. As far as I can see, they are more concerned with institutionalizing markets than with "taming capitalism." They want legal security for investments – in other words, an effective international equivalent for what civil law provides within the national context. However, creating and institutionalizing new markets is always easier than correcting them. Hard problems call for supranational harmonization of environmental, social, and economic policies.

Question: The politicians' energy was barely sufficient to ensure the introduction of the Euro. On what do you base your hope that a

European project will somehow keep pace with economic developments?

J. H.: Well, even Kohl shifted to a Europe of Fatherlands after the Cardiff conference. The historical motivation of the postwar generations – overcoming a murderous nationalism and reconciliation with France – now seems to be spent. But Delors' struggle for a "social dimension" is fueled by other, more immediate motives. That's why Joschka Fischer will be the more reliable European in the future. I have known him for long enough and well enough – the handover of European politicy from Kohl to Fischer is a stroke of luck. Granted, the attitude toward Brussels among the population in many European countries is quite negative. That is not just the case in Germany. Other nations have plenty of problems of their own. And the political elites pay no attention unless intellectuals manage to prompt at least a couple of public debates. But they don't, even less so here than in France and Britain. Your skepticism is, unfortunately, well founded.

Question: Assuming that a European political union came about, who should control it? Would you settle for a "disarmed" democracy, one without a critical public sphere?

J. H.: No. I support a European federal state, and that means a European constitution. Of course, such institutions, which currently exist only on the drawing board, can at best initiate the processes through which they acquire a foundation. A common political culture can't be conjured up out of nothing; nor is it generated spontaneously by favorable economic conditions. But a European constitution and a European party system are worthwhile aspirations. Associations, initiatives, and civic movements reaching across national borders – in other words, a European civil society – can only develop with the successful formation of a European public sphere. That's the crucial point. But this project is not condemned to failure by Europe's linguistic pluralism, as the German Federal Constitutional Court felt called upon to proclaim in its Maastricht decision. The school systems in the Scandinavian countries and the Netherlands are already fostering bilingualism. Why should English as a common "second first language" be precluded by the narcissism of the larger nations?

Question: Once again you're harboring illusions about the media society.

J. H.: Ah, yes, the media society. There's something refreshingly egalitarian about the debunking of the sublime – a flop is a flop. Still, if everything gets turned into a TV talk show, if everyone becomes a talk-show host talking only to other talk-show hosts, then the world takes on a Luhmannian cast. I don't think that I harbor any illusions about the state of a public sphere that takes its cues from the commercialized mass media. There have been many attempts to theorize this virtual reality. But in *Between Facts and Norms* I examined it from an entirely different viewpoint . . .

Question: . . . that of the democratic sovereign.

J. H.: Yes. For our constitution still expresses the idea of a self-legislating democratic community. The bare proposition that all state power derives from the people may not say much about actual conditions, but still it's not nothing. For example, citizens wouldn't turn out to vote if they were not at least intuitively convinced that the established procedures had something to do with the classical idea of democratic self-determination. The pressing question is whether this idea can be interpreted in a way that prevents it from being cynically emptied of content or from foundering on the realities of highly complex societies. Communication via the mass media plays an important role in the normative vision I advocate. A dispersed public interconnected almost exclusively through the electronic media can keep up to date on all kinds of issues and contributions in the mass media with a minimum of attention, even in fleeting moments during the day, in small, private circles. People can take affirmative or negative positions on issues, and they do this implicitly all the time. In this way, they contribute to evaluating competing public opinions, if not to their articulation. Public communication operates as a hinge between informal opinion-formation and the institutionalized processes of will-formation – a general election or a cabinet meeting, for example. For this reason, the discursive constitution of the public sphere is important.

Question: But even state-funded public television isn't discursive anymore.

J. H.: It's true that the political public sphere is part of a broader cultural public sphere, and today both are connected to the polluted
channels of commercial television. What's worse, public TV is competing against the most debased programming and formats of commercial television in a race to the bottom. The state-financed public
television format certainly has its problems. But it was inspired by
the right idea, namely, that not all important domains of social life
can be transferred to the market without loss. Culture, information,
and criticism depend on a distinctive form of elaborated communication. The dictates of ratings should not be allowed to seep into the
very pores of cultural communication. But there is nothing new in
this.

Question: That prompts the question of the future of party-based
democracy, which depends on an intact public sphere. Aren't we currently witnessing the gradual demise of party-based democracy? The
political parties are fulfilling less and less the function of sites in
which politics is conducted and issues are politicized. At the same
time, the social milieus that fostered adherence to political parties
are disintegrating.

J. H.: Political scientists have described these trends very well. They
are by no means entirely new, if you think of Lazarsfeld's radio
research from the early 1940s. But the media-driven personalization
of politics, the direct contact of leading politicians with the viewing
public, does intensify the plebiscitary element considerably and
diminishes the importance of the party organizations. Externally
directed public relations would still overshadow the internal communication among members even if the party's task of political per-
suasion had not been diluted into a marketing exercise. On the other
hand, one should take a close look at the younger generations. Today,
the broader population is more intelligent, at any rate better educated, better informed, and in many respects even more engaged,
than before. Changes in forms of political participation aren't in
and of themselves harmful. Although it is true that political parties
are becoming increasingly integrated into the state apparatus, while
at the same time marketing their activities increasingly aggressively,
countervailing movements can arise within civil society. The Greens
followed the classic path from a social movement to a political party.
But this is not the only possibility. Other initiatives remain in the

more fluid state of oppositional movements and organizations. And some of them, like Greenpeace, even manage to exert global influence.

Question: Assuming that party-based democracy were to dissolve, then both the old and the new public spheres would come under pressure to adapt. New movements would emerge. But in order to take advantage of the resulting opportunities, the rules of the media game would have to be rewritten. The form of media-based democracy in the United States does not provide an encouraging example. What form could the new rules of the media game take?

J. H.: That's a good question, and one to which I don't have an answer. I haven't thought about it sufficiently. However, party-based democracy in Europe is by no means a thing of the past. After all, the parties still select and train the political personnel. The level of professionalism among our politicians isn't all that bad. There has to be room for political opportunists, but God save us from dazzling figures like Berlusconi and Ross Perot, who appear out of nowhere.

Question: One can readily agree that there are mental blockages and self-blockages in the structurally conservative Federal Republic. Is Germany clinging too doggedly to its own past, to the egalitarian game-rules? What ballast should it throw overboard?

J. H.: It may well be that the German mentality following the ruptures German society experienced during the twentieth century is a bit too conservative. But I am leery of the supposed ballast of the welfare state which the neoliberals would have us jettison. "Greater flexibility" boils down to stripping labor of its specifically human attributes and reducing it to a normal commodity. But didn't Marx teach us not to confuse labor with commodities? Of course, there are mental blockages. At a time of national unification, it's hard for many Germans to grasp the fact that the era of the nation-state is coming to a close. Others want to repress the issue of the end of the full-employment society and how the reduced volume of wage labor should be redistributed. Now that capitalism as a mode of production of social wealth has prevailed worldwide, the old questions of distributive justice return – questions concerning the use of wage labor as the mechanism of distribution.

Question: Do you share Richard Sennett's concern that the end of the century is witnessing a new form of adaptation to capitalism? Will the "flexible man" become the new role model?

J. H.: Sennett's description of the individualization of social burdens is very insightful. His "flexible man" is the type of person onto whose shoulders society shifts the problems it doesn't manage to solve itself.

Question: Currently, there are proposals to uncouple democracy from justice and to emphasize only liberties or negative freedoms at the expense of social rights. Ralf Dahrendorf, for example, now seems to regard only "inclusion" as important, but not distributive justice. Then there are cynics who see the role of the state as residing exclusively in preparing individuals for a "market-ready" existence. What do you make of this new realism?

J. H.: I don't know exactly what Dahrendorf means by "inclusion." But you're right: a normative brainwashing that questions the universalistic foundations of the 200-year-old egalitarian self-understanding of modernity is currently all the rage. In Germany, this is coming from the conservative rather than the liberal side. We have a strong tradition of anthropological pessimism. It surveys the history of the hierarchical societies and fatalistic mentalities of the ancient empires and lectures us about the "egalitarian illusions" of a brief historical epoch based on a fundamental misunderstanding of human nature. It's a view that fits well with skepticism toward all attempts to reregulate out-of-control markets. If we follow the worldview of the neoliberal experts to its logical conclusion, it is understandable why highly mobile individuals, caught up in norm-free socioeconomic networks and guided only by their own preferences, might succumb to fatalism concerning an environment that completely escapes their control. It could become the secular counterpart of the religious fatalism of the old high cultures.

Question: Still, this praise for individual entrepreneurship reflects a new realism. The "Berlin generation" stands tragically alone and has solidarity only with itself. Perhaps it feels that after all the pressures toward individualism, there's no longer any such thing as civil society. Political existentialism seems a more attractive option than democratic experimentalism.

J. H.: My friend Herbert Marcuse, who never lost his Berlin inflection even in English, would have had a straightforward response to the current cant about the "Berlin generation": "shit with liquorice." You can't simply proclaim a new generation or a new culture, however much we might desire it for the new capital. A new generation arises by producing something new – a design is not enough. And it's not as if we didn't know what is required. Cultural criticism lacks a new, trenchant language – a language in which we could skewer the new developments as uncompromisingly as Adorno did those in the early years of the Federal Republic. Botho Strauss's *The Copyist's Errors* merely reflects the dulled sensibility of intellectuals who once again don the toga of "the learned."

You also allude to the sentiments which find expression in attempts at self-definition and self-discovery. That's more interesting. Young conservative attitudes certainly rose to the surface and popped like soap bubbles during the postwar decades, especially in hothouses like the feuilleton of the *Frankfurter Allgemeine Zeitung.* The resentment of our pre-eminent right-wing intellectuals, who saw themselves as the bearers of authentic German continuities but did not achieve very much after 1945, has left indelible traces in the political and intellectual history of the Federal Republic. At any rate, these circles cultivated the view that the cultural orientation of the Federal Republic to the West had cut us off from the roots of our authentic "Germanness." This consciousness, which again became virulent after 1989, found a single offensive outlet in the "New Right's" campaign to recover the nation's "self-consciousness." But this attempt failed with the 1995 debate over the retrospective meaning of the German surrender on May 8, 1945. Evidently, similarly warped needs are now seeking other, less blatant outlets. But I am not in a good position to judge this.

Question: Toward the end of his tenure, Helmut Kohl gave the impression that he wanted to exorcise the ghosts of the "Berlin Republic" as quickly as they were conjured up by his eager political advisors. Berlin remains Bonn. Was he frightened by his own daring?

J. H.: Just be happy that Schröder also emphasized the continuities between Bonn and Berlin following the election.

Question: That's not so obvious. The political fronts have almost been reversed. Now the SPD has discovered culture and rhapsodizes about the new, trend-setting capital and enthuses about building a replica of the Stadtschloss, while turning its back on the construction of a Holocaust memorial.[6] Why is the Cinderella culture suddenly all the rage?

J. H.: It's hard to say what the point of Schröder's publicity stunt is. Maybe it's harmless. In a tough economy, media-effective but cost-free policies are popular. Blair has discovered constitutional reform; with Schröder I'm afraid it's culture. But it's a tricky road to go down, as your examples show. And there are costs. Do we really want to leave the fate of a civilized country's rich cultural infrastructure to corporate sponsors? A closer look at the example of the United States is rather sobering. And as regards the representation of Germany's historically strongly regionalized culture abroad, the Goethe Institute is doing a very good job.

Question: The opening of our culture toward the West is constantly being criticized. For example, there's the fear that in philosophy, continental or specifically German traditions are being pushed into the background in favor of Anglo-American issues and perspectives. Do you share this concern?

J. H.: For postwar philosophy in Germany, the close connections with Anglo-American philosophy initiated by the emigrants led to an opening and an enormous enrichment. As the pioneering role played by my friend Karl-Otto Apel shows, the vigorous appropriation of analytic philosophy and American pragmatism generated new impulses without damaging the substance of the German tradition. And the exchange works in both directions. Richard Rorty's student Bob Brandom is in the process of cracking the Hegelian safe with analytical tools. Rorty himself is, of course, a brilliant analytic philosopher. But his international reputation is based on a synthetic style of appropriating issues and contexts which can be traced to the Hegelian roots of American pragmatism.

Question: Since you wish to appropriate the term "Berlin Republic," what continuities with the traditions of the Federal Republic do you think are indispensable?

J. H.: I believe that we all would like to live in a civilized country which has opened itself up in a cosmopolitan manner and takes its place among the other nations in a cautious and cooperative spirit. We would all like to be surrounded by fellow citizens who are accustomed to respecting the integrity of foreigners, the autonomy of individuals, and diversity, be it regional, ethnic, or religious. Moreover, the new Republic would do well to remember Germany's role in the catastrophic history of the twentieth century, but also to preserve the memory of those rare moments of emancipation and the achievements of which we can be justly proud. Quite unoriginally, I would wish for a mentality that is suspicious of high-flown rhetoric and rejects the aestheticization of politics, while remaining alert to the limits of trivialization when it comes to the integrity and the distinctiveness of intellectual creations.

Part II

Interventions

Three weeks into the controversial NATO military action, I took a stance on the Kosovo conflict (in *Die Zeit*, April 29, 1999). Aspects of the operation that had been problematic from the beginning – the paper-thin legitimacy according to international law, the disproportionate use of military force and the unclear political objectives – were thrown into even sharper relief by the subsequent course of events and the facts which have since come to light. Nevertheless, I still defend the Kantian perspective of a transition from international to cosmopolitan law from which I sought to justify the intervention in principle at the time.

My retrospective commentary on the CDU political donations scandal, which originally appeared in the March 18–19, 2000 issue of the *Süddeutschen Zeitung*, shows how normative consciousness can crumble at the heart of society.

Prior to the decision of the Federal Parliament to erect the Berlin memorial for the murdered European Jews, I again addressed the question of how this unusual undertaking should be interpreted (in *Die Zeit*, March 31, 1999).

2

From Power Politics to Cosmopolitan Society

With the first military engagement of the German Bundeswehr, the long period of self-restraint which shaped the civic features of the postwar German mentality came to a close. This is a war. The "air strikes" of the alliance are certainly meant to be different from war in the traditional mold. And the "surgical precision" of the air attacks and the policy of avoiding civilian casualties do indeed have a high legitimating value. They signify the rejection of the idea of total war which marked the physiognomy of the century now coming to a close. But even we semi-participants, with our nightly helpings of the Kosovo conflict on television, know that the Yugoslav population racing for cover from aerial bombardments is experiencing nothing other than war.

Fortunately, the portentous tones have been missing from the German public debates. No longing for fate, no intellectual drum rolls for the brave comrades in arms. During the Gulf War, the rhetoric of a national emergency and invocations of state pathos, dignity, tragedy, and manly courage were still being marshaled against a vociferous peace movement. Not much remains of either this time. Here and there some gloating over the now-muted pacifists, or the provocation "We've climbed down from our moral high horse." But not even this strikes the right tone, because both supporters and opponents of the Kosovo intervention alike are using a crystal-clear normative language.

Pacifists opposed to the war appeal to the moral distinction between action and omission and highlight the suffering of civilians which is the "inevitable side-effect" of even the most precise uses of military force. But this time their appeal is not aimed at the consciences of uncompromising realists who cling tenaciously to *raison d'état*. Instead, it's directed against the "legal pacifism" of the Red-Green government. Side by side with the old democracies which have been more deeply influenced than Germany by the modern natural law tradition, ministers Fischer and Scharping are invoking the idea of a domestication of the state of nature between states by means of human rights.[1] And in doing so, they have put the transformation of international law into cosmopolitan law on the political agenda.

Legal pacifism does not merely aim at containing the latent state of war between sovereign states through international law; it wants to overcome it entirely though a cosmopolitan order based on law. From Kant to Kelsen, Germany has also shared in this tradition. But it is now being taken seriously by a German government for the first time. Direct membership in an association of world citizens would protect citizens even against the arbitrary acts of their own government. As the Pinochet case already shows, the most important consequence of a law that bypasses state sovereignty is the personal liability of officials for crimes committed in the service of the state and the military.

In Germany, the public controversy over the Kosovo intervention is dominated by moral pacifists, on the one side, and legal pacifists, on the other. Even the "realists" have donned the mantle of normative rhetoric. Of course, the pro and con positions bring together contradictory motives. Those who think in terms of power politics and mistrust any normative restraints on sovereign state power on principle find themselves arm-in-arm with pacifists. The "Atlanticists," by contrast, suppress their suspicion of the government's enthusiasm for human rights – their suspicion of people who not so long ago took to the streets in protest against the stationing of Pershing II missiles on German soil – out of sheer loyalty to the allies. Dregger and Bahr stand alongside Stroeble; Schäuble and Rühe alongside Eppler.[2] In short, the Left in government, together with the primacy of normative arguments, explain not only the peculiar political alignments but also the reassuring fact that the public discussion and mood in Germany are no different from those in other Western European countries. No special German path or consciousness. If anything, fault lines are beginning to emerge between continental Europe and the United States and Britain, or at any rate between those who invite the UN Secretary General to their meetings and seek a *rapprochement* with Russia, and those who mainly trust in their own weapons.

War against Ethnic Cleansing

Of course, the United States and the member states of the European Union that bear the political responsibility for the intervention start from a common position. After the failed negotiations at Rambouillet, they are conducting the threatened punishment strikes against Yugoslavia with the declared goal of implementing a liberal solution for the autonomy of Kosovo within Serbia. Within the framework of classical international law, this would have counted as an interference in the internal affairs of a sovereign state, that is, as a violation of the principle of non-intervention. Premised on human rights policy, this intervention is now supposed to be regarded as an armed peace mission tacitly authorized by the international community – though without a UN mandate. According to this Western interpretation, the war in Kosovo could mark a significant advance on the road from classical international law between states to the cosmopolitan law of a society of world citizens.

This development began with the founding of the United Nations and, after a period of stagnation during the Cold War, it was accelerated by the 1991 Gulf War and other interventions. Since 1945, of course, humanitarian interventions have only been conducted in the name of the UN and with the official agreement of the government involved (assuming that a functioning state authority existed). During the Gulf War, the UN Security Council intervened de facto in the "internal affairs" of a sovereign state by establishing no-fly zones in Iraqi airspace and "safe havens" for Kurdish refugees in northern Iraq. But this was not explicitly justified by the need to protect a persecuted minority from its own government. In Resolution 688 of April 1991, the UN appealed to its right of intervention in cases of "a threat to international security." The current situation is different. NATO is acting without a mandate from the Security Council, but justifies its intervention as emergency aid for a persecuted ethnic (and religious) minority.

Some 300,000 people in Kosovo were already subjected to murder, terror, and expulsion in the months leading up to the air strikes. In the meantime, the horrific images of streams of refugees on the roads to Macedonia, Montenegro, and Albania provide irrefutable evidence of a carefully planned ethnic-cleansing operation. That the refugees are now being held as hostages does not make the situation any better. Although Milosevic is using the NATO air campaign to force his despicable policy through to the bitter end, the harrowing scenes from the refugee camps cannot disguise the true direction of the causal link. In the final analysis, the aim of the negotiations was to put a stop to this murderous ethno-nationalism. Whether the principles of the 1948 Convention on Genocide apply to what is now taking place under the cover of the air strikes is a matter of controversy. But there can be no doubt about which acts became "crimes against humanity" in international law in accordance with the guidelines of the war crimes tribunals in Nuremberg and Tokyo. Recently, the Security Council has also begun to treat these acts as "threats to peace," which can justify the use of force under certain circumstances. But in the absence of a mandate from the Security Council, in this case the coalition forces had to fall back on the *erga omnes* binding principles of international law to derive an authorization for the emergency action.

Be that as it may, the Kosovars' claim to equal rights and the outrage over the injustice of their brutal expulsion have earned broad, albeit differentiated, support for military intervention in the West. Karl Lamers, the foreign policy spokesperson of the CDU, gave voice to the ambivalence which has accompanied this support from the beginning: "Thus we could have an easy conscience. This is what our heads tell us, but in our hearts we are not really convinced. We are uncertain and uneasy . . ."

Nagging Doubts

There are ample reasons for disquiet. Over the past weeks, doubts about the *wisdom* of a negotiation strategy that left no alternative to armed attack have grown stronger. For doubts remain concerning the *utility* of the military strikes. While support for Milosevic's stubbornly defiant course is growing among the Yugoslav population even deep into the ranks of the opposition, the ominous side-effects of war are piling up all around. For a variety of reasons the bordering states of

Macedonia and Albania and the semi-republic of Montenegro are being sucked into the downward spiral of instability, whereas in Russia, with its large arsenal of nuclear weapons, widespread solidarity with the Slavic "brothers" is putting the government under increasing pressure. Above all, doubts are growing about the *proportionality* of the military measures. Behind every incident of "collateral damage" – every train unintentionally plunged into the Danube when a bridge is bombed, every tractor laden with fleeing Albanians, every Serbian neighborhood and civilian target unintentionally hit by a stray missile – lies not just a contingency of war but the human suffering that "our" intervention has on its conscience.

Questions of proportionality are hard to decide. Shouldn't NATO have issued an advance warning half an hour before destroying the state broadcasting service? Even the intentional acts of destruction – the cigarette factory and gasworks in flames, the bombed-out skyscrapers, roads and bridges, the destruction of the economic infrastructure of a nation already suffering under the UN embargo – add to the disquiet. Every child who dies in flight plagues our conscience. For despite the transparent causal connections, the threads of responsibility are becoming entangled. In the misery of the mass expulsions, the consequences of the ruthless policies of a state terrorist combine with the side-effects of military attacks – which instead of putting a stop to his bloody handiwork provide him with an additional pretext to continue it – to form a tangled knot.

Finally, there are doubts concerning the increasing *vagueness* of the political objectives of the intervention. Certainly, the five basic demands made on Milosevic are informed by the same impeccable principles as the Dayton Accord for a liberal, multi-ethnic Bosnia. The Kosovar Albanians would have no right to secede provided that their claim to autonomy within Serbia was fulfilled. The Greater Albanian nationalism that would be promoted by a secession is not one jot better than the Greater Serbian nationalism the intervention was meant to check. Meanwhile, with each passing day the wounds of ethnic cleansing make it ever more urgent to revise the earlier goal of an equal coexistence of the different ethnic groups. Yet the partition of Kosovo would be a true secession, something which nobody can want. Moreover, the establishment of a protectorate would require a change in strategy, namely, a ground war and the decades-long presence of peacekeeping troops. Should these unforeseen consequences materialize, the question of the legitimacy of the whole undertaking would again take on an entirely different appearance in hindsight.

There is a certain shrillness in the pronouncements of our own government, an overkill with dubious historical comparisons – as though Fischer and Scharping needed to drown out a *different* inner voice with their insistent rhetoric. Is it the fear that the political failure of the military operation could cast a completely different light on the intervention, and even set the project of the thorough-going juridification of international relations back by decades? And, if so, would all that remained of the "police action" which NATO is magnanimously conducting on behalf of the international community be an ordinary war, even a dirty war, that has plunged the Balkans into even greater chaos? And wouldn't this be grist for the mill of a Carl Schmitt, who always knew better: "Whoever speaks of 'humanity' is a liar"? Schmitt expressed his anti-humanism in the famous formula, "Humanity, bestiality." Among all the sources of disquiet, the gnawing doubt that legal pacifism itself might be the wrong project cuts the deepest.

The Contradictions of *Realpolitik* . . .

The war in Kosovo touches on a fundamental question that is hotly disputed in political science and philosophy. The constitutional state accomplished the tremendous civilizing task of legally taming political power on the basis of the recognition of the sovereignty of the collective subjects of international law, whereas a "cosmopolitan condition" would place the independence of nation-states in question. Does the universalism of the Enlightenment here collide with a stubborn form of political power that is indelibly inscribed with the drive for collective self-assertion of a particular community? This is the realist thorn in the flesh of human rights politics.

Of course, even the realist school cannot ignore the structural transformation of the system of independent states that emerged with the Peace of Westphalia in 1648: the interdependencies of an increasingly complex world society; the sheer scale of the problems which states can solve only through cooperation; the growing authority and density of supranational institutions, regimes and procedures, not only in the field of collective security; the economization of foreign policy and, in general, the blurring of the classical boundary between domestic and foreign policy. But a pessimistic image of human nature and a peculiarly opaque conception of "the" political form the background of a doctrine that clings more or less unconditionally to the principle of non-intervention. According to this doctrine, independent nation-states in the international state of nature should act freely in accordance with their own interests because the security and survival of the collective are non-negotiable values for its members and because, from the point of view of an observer, conflicts between collective actors are still best regulated by the imperatives of instrumental rationality.

From this viewpoint, interventionist human rights policy commits a category mistake. It underestimates and stigmatizes the "natural" tendency of states toward self-assertion. It tries to impose normative criteria on a potential for violence which escapes normative regulation. Carl Schmitt sharpened this line of argument still further with his peculiar essentialist conception of the political. With its attempt to "moralize" an essentially neutral *raison d'état*, Schmitt argued, the politics of human rights itself causes the quasi-natural struggle between nations to degenerate into an unholy "struggle against evil."

This position is open to convincing objections. It is not as if in the postnational constellation muscular nation-states would be tied down by rules of the international community. On the contrary, it is the erosion of state authority, civil wars, and ethnic conflicts within imploding states or repressive societies which create the need for interventions in the first place – not only in Somalia and Rwanda, but also in Bosnia and now in Kosovo. Nor is the suspicion that the politics of human rights is a mere ideological mask very convincing. The current situation shows that universalist forms of justification by no means *always* conceal particular interests. The hermeneutics of suspicion makes a rather poor case against the present intervention. For politicians robbed of much of their domestic scope for action by the global economy, muscle-flexing in foreign affairs may be an attractive option. But neither the aim of securing and expanding its spheres of influence attributed to the United States, nor the aim of finding a new role ascribed to NATO, nor even the aim of a pre-emptive defence against waves of immigration ascribed to "Fortress Europe," can explain the decision to undertake such a momentous, risky, and costly intervention.

The principal fact which speaks against "realism," however, is that the subjects of international law, by drawing a bloody trail of destruction across the catastrophic history of the twentieth century, have made a mockery of the presumption of moral indifference accorded them by classical international law. The foundation of the United Nations and the UN Declaration of Human Rights, as well as the threat to punish wars of aggression and crimes against humanity (resulting in at least a half-hearted restriction of the principle of non-intervention) – these were necessary and proper responses to the morally significant experiences of the twentieth century, that is, to political totalitarianism and the Holocaust.

. . . and the Dilemma of Human Rights Politics

The reproach of a moralization of politics ultimately rests on a conceptual confusion. For the establishment of a cosmopolitan order would not mean that violations of human rights would be judged and combated *immediately* in accordance with moral standards; instead, they would be prosecuted like criminal acts within national legal systems. A thorough juridification of international relations is not possible without established procedures for resolving conflicts. The institutionalization of these legal procedures will itself preserve the judicial processing of human rights violations against a moral de-differentiation of law and prevent an *unmediated* moral stigmatization of "enemies."

Achieving such a cosmopolitan condition does not require a world state that enjoys a monopoly on the means of violence or a global government. The minimum requirements, however, are a functioning Security Council, the binding jurisdiction of an international criminal court and the complementing of the General Assembly of government representatives by a "second chamber" made up of representatives of world citizens. Since these reforms of the United Nations are still a long way off, insisting on the distinction between juridification and moralization remains a correct, but double-edged response. For as long as human rights are comparatively weakly institutionalized at the global level, the boundary between law and morality can easily become blurred, as we see in the present case. With a deadlocked Security Council, NATO can only appeal to the moral validity of international law – to norms for which no effective, internationally recognized institutions of application and enforcement exist.

The under-institutionalization of cosmopolitan law is reflected, for example, in the yawning gap between the legitimacy of peacekeeping and peacemaking interventions and their effectiveness. The UN declared Srebrenica to be a safe haven, but the forces legitimately stationed there were unable to prevent the gruesome massacre which followed the Serbian invasion. On the other hand, NATO can only effectively oppose the Yugoslav government because it acted without the legitimation which the Security Council would have refused to grant.

The politics of human rights aims to close the gap between these mirror-image situations. But given the under-institutionalization of cosmopolitan law, such a politics is in many respects compelled to become a mere *anticipation* of the future cosmopolitan condition which it simultaneously seeks to realize. How can one conduct a politics that is supposed to secure equal respect for human rights, if necessary with military force, under these paradoxical circumstances? This question does not lose its relevance just because we cannot intervene everywhere, for example, on behalf of the Kurds, or the Chechens, or the Tibetans, but only on our own doorstep in the war-torn Balkans. Here an interesting difference in the interpretation of human rights politics is emerging between Americans and Europeans. The United States is promoting the global implementation of human rights as the national mission of a superpower that pursues this goal under the premises of power politics. Most of the EU governments, by contrast, understand human rights politics as the project of establishing the rule of law in international relations which is already transforming the parameters of power politics.

In a world of states only weakly regulated by the UN, the United States has taken upon itself the regulatory tasks of a superpower. Human rights thereby function as moral value orientations for assessing political goals. Of course, there have always been isolationist countercurrents in the United States and, like other nations, it has always given priority to its own interests, which are not always in harmony with its declared normative goals. This was demonstrated by the Vietnam War, and repeatedly by its handling of problems in its own "backyard." But the "new hybrid of humanitarian selflessness

and the logic of imperialist power politics" (Ulrich Beck) actually has
a long tradition in the United States. Among Wilson's motives for
entering World War I, and Roosevelt's for entering World War II, were
ideals deeply rooted in the pragmatist tradition. We have these ideals
to thank for the fact that our defeat in 1945 was also our liberation.
From this very American, hence national, perspective of a normatively oriented power politics, it must seem plausible to pursue the
struggle against Yugoslavia, regardless of complications, steadfastly
and uncompromisingly, if necessary with the deployment of ground
forces. This option has at least the merit of consistency. But what
would we say if, one day, a military alliance from another region –
let us say Asia – were to pursue an armed human rights politics
resting on an entirely different interpretation – their interpretation –
of international law and the UN Charter?

Inhibitions to Paternalism

Things appear quite different if human rights are treated not just as
a moral guide for unilateral political actions but as rights which must
be implemented in the legal sense. For notwithstanding their purely
moral content, human rights exhibit the structural features of individual rights which are essentially oriented to achieving positive
validity within an established legal order. Only when human rights
have found their proper "place" in a global democratic constitutional
order, analogous to that of the basic rights in our national constitutions, will we be able to assume that the addressees of these rights
can also regard themselves as their authors at the global level. The
institutions of the United Nations are on a course to close the circle
between the enforcement of binding law and democratic law-making.
Where this has not been achieved, norms remain *forcibly imposed*
constraints, however moral their content. Certainly, the intervening
states are trying to enforce the claims of all those in Kosovo whose
human rights are being trampled upon by their own government.
However, the Serbs who are dancing in the streets of Belgrade are
not, as Slavoj Zizek remarks, "Americans in disguise, waiting to be
freed from the curse of nationalism." A political order guaranteeing
equal rights for all citizens is being imposed upon them by force of

arms. This is also true from a normative perspective, at least as long as the UN has not taken a formal decision on military sanctions against its member Yugoslavia.

Even 19 undoubtedly democratic states, as long as they authorize their own intervention, remain partisan. They are exercising a power of interpretation and decision-making which, if things were properly conducted, could only be exercised by independent institutions. To this extent, they are acting paternalistically. There are good moral reasons for this. But whoever acts with an awareness of the temporary unavoidability of paternalism also knows that the force they exercise does not yet possess the character of a legal coercion legitimated by a democratic cosmopolitan order. Moral norms which appeal to our better judgment may not be enforced like established legal norms.

But the dilemma of having to act as if the goal of a fully institutionalized cosmopolitan order were already realized does not entail the maxim of abandoning victims to their persecutors. The terroristic misuse of state power transforms a classic civil war into a mass crime. When there is no other way, democratic neighboring states must be permitted to intervene in an emergency in accordance with customary international law. But in such cases the incompleteness of the cosmopolitan condition demands exceptional sensitivity. The existing institutions and procedures are the only available controls on the fallible judgments of a partisan actor who presumes to act on behalf of all.

One source of misunderstandings is, for example, the historical non-simultaneity of clashing political mentalities. There is not a 400-year time lag between NATO's aerial war and the Serb's ground war, as Hans Magnus Enzensberger seems to think. Greater Serbian nationalism is more reminiscent of Ernst-Moritz Arndt than of Grimmelshausen.[3] But political scientists have shown that the difference between "first" and "second" worlds has re-emerged in a new form. Only the peaceful and prosperous OECD societies can afford the luxury of bringing their national interests more or less in line with the halfway-cosmopolitan expectations of the United Nations. By contrast, the "second world" (on the new reading) is the heir to the power politics of European nationalism. States such as Libya, Iraq, or Serbia compensate for their internal instability through authoritarian rule and identity politics, whereas in foreign policy they are expansionist, touchy about border issues, and neurotically defend their sovereignty. Such observations tend to reinforce inhibitions in interactions among states. Today they support calls for strengthening diplomatic efforts.

It is one thing for the United States to instrumentalize human rights by playing the role of hegemonic guarantor of global order in accordance with its political traditions, however admirable these may be. It is quite another for us to understand the precarious transition from classical power politics to a cosmopolitan order, beyond the divisions of the current military conflict, as a learning process to be mastered collectively. This more comprehensive perspective also calls for greater caution. The self-empowerment of NATO should not become the rule.

3

A Sort of Logo of
the Free West

The scandal over the illegal political donations to the CDU is now on the wane. The presidium of the CDU has steeled itself to some constructive measures and further revelations from Wiesbaden are generating only mild interest. The mills of the public prosecutor's office and the parliamentary investigative committees are grinding slowly. All that remains is a certain disquiet over the strange disproportion between the magnitude of the affair and the insignificance of its consequences. Is Schäuble the only loser? The rising din in the media followed by its fading without a sound is, of course, the typical pattern of political scandals. And didn't this affair have all the hallmarks of a perfectly ordinary scandal?

The affair began innocuously enough with the Augsburg arrest warrant for Walther Leisler Kiep, the former treasurer of the CDU, on November 14.[1] With the confessions of ex-Chancellor Helmut Kohl and his interior minister a month later, it acquired sufficient momentum to undermine the reputation of a national party, sweep its incumbent chairman, Wolfgang Schäuble, from office, overshadow a state parliamentary election, and threaten to bring down a state government. Honorable men were unmasked as crooks. Events unfolded in the rhythm of a farce: the stalling tactics of the main players as the details were squeezed out of them drop by drop by the prosecutors and the media; the supporting roles played by the informant and blackmailer in a Canadian hideout, the meticulously crooked accountant in the town house, and the state secretary who went underground in Bangkok, among others; the international network connecting prominent politicians and officials with shady lobbyists and agents; and the cross-border system of numbered accounts and foundations with imposing names. And let us not forget the fiendishly clever trick of camouflaging illegal transfers as "Jewish bequests," or the juicy details dug up by the Bild reporters – suitcases bulging with cash changing hands, stacks of banknotes from Munich businesses stashed under the bedspread at an exclusive Zurich hotel, or the safe lovingly described by the CDU financial advisor as "the size of a walk-in closet" (*Süddeutsche Zeitung*, March 4–5, 2000).

Not Your Usual Scandal

On the other hand, the spectacle lacks one of the typical features of garden-variety scandals – the clear-cut character of the triggering event. Folk psychology and everyday moral conceptions generally suffice for judging the human foibles at work in such affairs, with the result that the public reaction typically dissipates itself in outrage from which we learn nothing new. The wave of indignation clears the air only by reinforcing existing norms. Those implicated in the scandal are well advised not to contradict the prevailing consensus. In this respect, the political donations scandal is not your usual scandal. What is striking is the truly bizarre obtuseness of the main participants. The absence of any sense of guilt among the culprits is clearly echoed by the complaints of party cronies over poor crisis-management, as though the fallout could have been contained by clever public relations. Even the public is divided. In Schleswig-Holstein, the sense of disgust among CDU voters remained within bounds. In Hamburg and Bremen high society, Kohl's solemn oath, which is covering up violations of the law, met with undisguised approval. So is the fall from grace of a worthy "statesman" all that is at stake here?

Manfred Kanther, who juggled funds of dubious provenance among numbered accounts, cited the need to end a "witch hunt" as his reason for resigning. Kohl, whose actions violated both constitutional and criminal law, resigned his post as honorary chairman only at the urging of the party presidium. He accepted "political responsibility" for a "mistake" without drawing the logical conclusion and resigning his seat in parliament. Koch, who falsified official reports, confessed his "stupidity" and cheerfully continued as before. The behavior of apologizing without suffering consequences and the mentality of the co-conspirators caught up in the web of intrigue would be incomprehensible if this were a completely normal, limited affair. There can certainly be no quibbling over the criminality of using funds of dubious provenance to maintain political power. The applicable laws are equally clear – Article 21, Paragraph 1, Clause 4 of the Basic Law and the relevant laws governing political parties. Nevertheless, the relevance and seriousness of the affair remain matters of controversy. We must ask ourselves what affair we are actually dealing with here.

What Crisis?

Scandals are always fed by gossip and idle conversation. Yet no one has anything interesting to say because everyone agrees about the nature of the scandalous conduct and that the violation of the norms in question is wrong. But this scandal was different. Commentators felt immediately called upon to investigate the crises which were assumed to underlie the scandal. Even interventions by people always on the lookout for an excuse to ride their hobbyhorses – for example, the introduction of a first-past-the-post electoral system or a presidential system – attest to a certain need for interpretation. On the other hand, even the more serious interpretations have not identified problems that have contributed anything much to explaining the phenomenon, aside from the need to reform the statutes of the federal CDU.

Some commentators think that the appropriate response to the "party funding crisis" is to improve the laws governing political parties. But Hans Peter Bull rightly asks what such reforms would accomplish, "if those who have already violated existing law show no sense of guilt and are not prepared to meet their obligations even retrospectively." Others locate the crisis one level deeper and call for "the dismantling of the party state and the restitution of a vital party democracy" in order to restore the importance of state offices. But a "substantial" state which operates independently from the democratic parties would not guarantee the neutral exercise of power. Moreover, when it comes to the undesirable trend toward the assimilation of the state and political parties which has been going on for decades,

the entanglements of the West-Landesbank with the state government of North Rhine-Westphalia in Düsseldorf are more significant
than the financial dealings of Kohl, Kanther, & Co.

The diagnosis which seeks to dig deeper by invoking the collapse
of conservatism is not any more convincing. Intellectuals of the
postwar transition such as Arnold Gehlen already adapted conservatism to the new conditions in the recently de-Nazified Federal
Republic. They laid the groundwork for the combination of strong
values and sustaining traditions with scientific and technical progress
and economic productivity which has proved to be so effective. The
neo-conservatives in 1970s simply added a social-welfare dimension
to this foundation, and it served as the original basis for Kohl's moral-
intellectual "turn." Stoiber and Koch are promoting a neoliberal
version of this same ideological division of labor with an aggressive
emphasis on national cultural identity.[2] They have been so successful that we have no need to worry about the mental reserves of the
conservative camp. But if all of these diagnoses of the crisis miss the
target, how can we explain the normative obliviousness of the actors
and the ambivalent reaction of the public?

The Scandal within the Scandal

Kohl's attempt to promote his own rehabilitation has failed. Let us
assume that Kohl wished to pre-empt his own party's demands for
compensation and to make good the 6.3 million Deutschmark loss
which, by his own calculation, he caused the party. He would have
had to pay this sum personally, either from his own resources, or by
taking out a loan, or through gifts from friends. On the other hand,
if his intention was to lend effective support to the not very successful fundraising efforts of his party, he would have had to ask his
friends discretely to support the plundered CDU through legal donations. Instead, Kohl chose a third path. He publicly cast himself in
the role of the powerful collector and dispenser of political donations. He wanted to demonstrate publicly that the donations are in
fact addressed to him as recipient, as gestures of solidarity with him
and his undeserved fate, even though they can only be legally donated
to the party. In this way, Kohl cast himself again as the Mafia boss
who flexes his muscles by transforming his social capital into cold

cash – all for the sake of the family, needless to say. And how does the CDU respond to this new humiliation? It puts a brave face on it and tamely accepts the money. Yet Kohl's chutzpah is accompanied by a chorus of voices of those eager to return to business as usual, warning the CDU not to don "penitential robes."

The whole episode must be understood in the context of the mentality which explains how a practice that is now criticized could be regarded as normal, or at worst as venial, in the past. I would hazard three conjectures, even though I have only weak evidence for the first. The fact that a form of conduct that is now illegal could continue even after the Flick affair may have to do with surreptitious practices concerning which we lack reliable information.[3] Tax evasion, which is regarded as a peccadillo in the business world, may simply have become the done thing, so to speak, in certain circles.

A more obvious explanation is the role of a brand of anti-communism that tends to translate differences in opinion in democratic controversies into fronts in a civil war. After all, the fact that many people viewed campaigns against "internal enemies" as an imperative of the times ensured that Carl Schmitt remained influential in the Federal Republic. Indeed, who could fail to become suspicious on learning from Horst Weyrauch that the CDU had sequestered documents relating to the funds it received from the Federal Intelligence Service to support foreign political parties in campaigns against leftist opponents in the same Zurich vault as records of (illegal?) donations?

Delayed Development

However, the most astonishing aspect of the affair is Kohl's and Kanther's normatively cavalier treatment of the constitution. Today, German historians are attempting to explain how the Federal Republic succeeded in building a stable democracy in spite of the overwhelming professional and intellectual continuities with the Nazi period. Of course, it took decades for the abstract principles of the constitution to take root in the attitudes and dispositions of the postwar generations. But even we alarmists, who remained mistrustful of this process into the 1980s, never dreamed that the constitution was apparently viewed in purely instrumental terms as a kind of logo for the "Free West" even by members of the political elite, rather than as a lived norm against which one should measure one's conduct as a matter of course. How else should we explain this peculiar form of "civil disobedience," which in reality is incompatible with the basic principles of the constitutional state because it rests on private notions of honor rather than on constitutional principles? Father Basilius Streithofen's scurrilous conception of natural law can no more salve Kohl of this stigma than the emergency legal aid which prominent law professors have spontaneously offered him. A violation of the constitution cannot be downplayed into a misdemeanor. Ernst-Wolfgang Böckenförde and Günter Frankenberg (in the *Frankfurter Allgemeine Zeitung* on February 14 and 22, 2000) have made the necessary corrections to their colleagues' selective reading of the constitution.

With hindsight, the subjective slackening of normative obligations may prove to be indicative of a delayed development of democratic consciousness in postwar Germany. Today, however, such fading motives from the past are encountering tendencies of an entirely different kind and origin which point in the same direction.

Two Interpretations of "Hypermorality"

The moral principles cited by the federal leadership of the FDP against the political maneuvering of party supporters in Hesse are suspected of being nothing more than a political strategy in normative disguise. One could read these commentaries as a warning against the destabilizing effects of moral criticism as such: "too much" morality is dangerous because it corrodes established practices and values. Such a naive neo-conservative dismissal of "hypermorality" acquires a different, postmodern spin when the insights of thinkers like Foucault or Luhmann are refashioned into the all-purpose cleansers of the opinionated. The political donations scandal has proved to be a glorious chapter in the history of investigative journalism, whose revelations depend on normative standards for their effects. But the new Nietzscheanism attempts to trump this *naïveté* by deconstructing all standards as such. From a truly critical perspective, in other words, politics is supposed to dissolve completely into its various scandals, where arguments serve only the function of media strategies guided by imperatives of power.

With the entry into the postmodern domain of virtual realities, we are told, distinctions between being and appearance, facticity and validity, true and false, lose their discriminating power. This project of intellectual de-differentiation would have no chance against the shrewd alliance of common sense and enlightenment had not politics itself abandoned its normative dimension, whether marching under the banner of neoliberalism or along Third Ways. A politics that surrenders its scope for action and its power to shape events, and submits itself to self-imposed systemic constraints, also turns its back on a central promise of modernity. It no longer presents itself as the medium in which a society can shape its destiny through the discursively generated and informed will of its united democratic citizenry. This is the hope which crumbles with the erosion of civic awareness of the binding character of norms.

4

The Finger of Blame: The Germans and Their Memorial

The Berlin Wall fell in November 1989. Around the same time, the "Society to Promote the Construction of a Memorial to the Murdered Jews of Europe" was recorded by the Registry of Associations. This initiative finally spurred the Parliament into action following a long period of procrastination. Now, almost a decade later, following two tenderings, numerous rounds of discussion, and the deadlock of last fall, the responsible parliamentary committee has held hearings on the why, where, and how of the central Holocaust memorial. The controversy sparked by Martin Walser marked a turning point.[1] His initiative backfired. On this occasion, political public opinion only managed to free itself from the gasses of an undigested past which emanate periodically from the stomach of the Federal Republic by virtue of the civil courage – this is what is disturbing – of a prominent Jew.

The federal Parliament is due to reach a final decision on the project before the summer recess. Let us not deceive ourselves. This is the first time in the 50-year history of the Federal Republic that a parliamentary vote for such a manifestly future-oriented sign of a purified German collective identity has moved into the realm of possibility. It also seems to be the last moment at which this is still possible. A Berlin Republic dedicated to the false, monumental past is looming ever larger . . .

Gerhard Schröder, who wishes to name the Reichstag building in Berlin, the future home of the federal Parliament, the "Reichstag,"[2] has taken issue with what he calls the "bad habit of pointing the finger of blame at the people," whereas others are already speaking of "discourse police." It is true that from Heuss and Heinemann to Herzog and Rau there has not only been a differentiation between levels of speech but also a filter separating published opinions, official language use, and formal speech, on the one hand, from popular prejudices and beer hall blather, on the other. This filter has occasionally trapped the wrong victims – think of poor Jenninger.[3] But it was also an essential precondition for the gradual emergence of a liberal political culture, which had to be fought for over deep domestic political divisions. Now it seems that the distinction between "Bundestag" and "Reichstag," which is rich in historical connotations, is to be leveled out. The incumbent Chancellor is set to go down in the later history of the republic – which happily learned from its achievements instead of crowing about them – as a leveler. Instead of a memorial that is designed to serve as an irritant, he prefers a pleasant city castle as a picturesque backdrop for the erasure of all differences that still make a difference.

The heated debate over the planned memorial has been conducted for years at a high level and with great seriousness. It has led to clarifications in both procedure and substance. There is now a consensus on the meaning and purpose of the memorial, whereas questions about its aesthetic form remain controversial, for good reasons. One important question remains open, namely: should the memorial be dedicated exclusively to the murdered Jews? Let us begin with the question of the project's meaning – who is expressing what by erecting this memorial? – and its objective – what purpose is it meant to serve and to whom is its message directed?

The Meaning of the Memorial

The catastrophic history of the twentieth century has stripped virtually all national traditions of their taken-for-granted character. Elsewhere, too, the collective identity of nations has become more fluid. Public controversies touched off by more or less contingent events – scandals and court cases, sensitive legislative matters, historical narratives, films, television series, and so on – impact on political self-understandings. This leads to controversies over the image that citizens have of their own country, of who they are and who they want to be. During the early years of the Federal Republic, there were numerous occasions of this sort: the rearmament policy, the case of Adenauer's advisor Globke, the screening of Veit Harlan films, the abduction of the Secret Service director John, the question of the statute of limitations for crimes committed during the Nazi years, the wearing of military decorations of the Third Reich, nuclear weapons for the Bundeswehr, and, of course, the first major Auschwitz trial in Frankfurt, which provided the subject matter for Peter Weiss's play *The Investigation*.[4]

Events such as these have multiplied right up to the present, with the debates over the involvement of the Wehrmacht in Nazi crimes, Daniel Goldhagen's book *Hitler's Willing Executioners*, and the complicity of banks and large corporations in Nazi extermination practices. By the same token, discussions have focused every more closely on *one* question which, in spite of its increasing virulence, nevertheless had a penetrating, mentality-shaping power from the very beginning: do we, the citizens of the Federal Republic of Germany, assume historical liability for the consequences of the actions of the "perpetrator generation" as the political, legal and cultural heirs to their state and society? Do we make the self-critical commemoration of "Auschwitz" – the attentive reflection on the events bound up with that name – into an explicit component of our political self-understanding? Do we accept the disturbing political responsibility that falls on later generations as a consequence of the breakdown in civilization, which was committed, supported, and tolerated by Germans, as an element of a fractured national identity? By "fractured" here is meant only that this responsibility implies the will to abandon habits of thought in the continuity of our own traditions that have led us astray. As descendants who remain liable, we tell ourselves "never again." The break in the continuity of our sustaining traditions is the precondition for recovering our self-respect.

If the planned memorial is to provide an answer to these questions, then its primary meaning cannot be that we remember Jewish victims also in the country of the perpetrators – that is, that we commemorate them in the same way as the descendants of the victims in Israel or the United States and thoughtful people throughout the world. It cannot be a matter of "us Germans giving the Jews a Holocaust memorial." The memorial must have another meaning in the context of our political culture. With this memorial, the present generation of descendants of the perpetrators profess a political self-understanding into which is branded the deed – the crime against humanity committed and tolerated under the National Socialist regime – and *therewith* the anguish over the unspeakable crimes inflicted upon its victims, as a permanent source of disquiet and admonition. In the recent hearings, this was called the "act and per-petrator-centered" meaning of the memorial.

Who Erects the Memorial?

With this, the circle of authors who could desire such a memorial closes. Neither Jewish Germans, nor the Sinti and Roma who reside in Germany, nor the immigrants who have become nationalized since the end of World War II, can say what this memo-rial should express. The authors are those citizens who are the direct heirs of a culture in which "that" was possible, who belong to a network of traditions that connects them with the perpetrator gen-eration. In erecting the memorial, they are simultaneously con-structing a relation to the perpetrators, to the victims, and to the victims' descendants.

Since we cannot know how we ourselves would have acted, a certain reserve in our moral judgments of the errors of our parents and grandparents is understandable as something more than the normal psychological inhibitions concerning those closest to us. As citizens of this country, we take an interest in the darkest chapter of our history – in the criminal behavior of the perpetrators and the problematic actions and omissions of the perpetrator generation – primarily as a means of critically reassuring ourselves of our own political identity. The willingness to recognize and acknowledge with the hindsight of history the true extent of guilt and complicity varies with our current understanding of freedom, that is, with how we understand ourselves as responsible persons and how much we demand of ourselves as political actors. How we retrospectively apportion blame and innocence, which was the political-ethical kernel of the Goldhagen controversy, also reflects the norms in terms of which we currently express our respect for each other as citizens of this republic.

The relation to a particular "we" is also grammatically inscribed in this process of collective self-understanding. On the other hand, the remembrance of the victims should not be simply treated as a means of achieving this self-awareness. The recollection of the mass murder is indeed located in the context of the political self-understanding of present-day generations. But an exclusive focus on what the deed and the perpetrators mean for us would inevitably hollow out the moral core of sympathy with the victims. The unconditional moral impulse to remember should not be relativized by the need for self-reassurance. We can only seriously commemorate the victims – and especially the victims – for their own sake. This was the correct, if incomplete, intuition that originally guided the sponsors of the initiative.

The value of the weak, indeed vain, force of anamnestic solidarity is truly lost if the self-reference takes on an independent narcissistic life of its own and the memorial [*Denkmal*] becomes a "mark of shame" [*Schandmal*].[5] Anyone who views Auschwitz as "our shame" is more interested in the image others have of us than in the image German citizens retrospectively form of themselves in view of the breakdown in civilization, which enables them to look each other in the face and show each other respect.

The memorial for the murdered Jews is an attempt to come to terms with ourselves. The aim is not to fulfill the expectations of contemporaries, whether inside or outside of Germany. The past separates the descendants of the perpetrators from those of the victims. This divided past will continue to hinder the cooperation of citizens in the present unless the one side takes a credible stand for conditions which make a shared life possible, even bearable, for the other side. A Holocaust memorial is also the expression of this civility toward the descendants of the victims.

Allowing for the delicate distribution of roles, our Jewish fellow-citizens have been productive participants in this debate. More recently naturalized immigrants, who belong neither to one side nor the other, are not immediately affected by it. Nevertheless, in becoming naturalized citizens, they accepted a political culture in full awareness of its historical burdens. They may well regard other things as relevant and will one day leave their own mark on the cultural memory of the nation. But, for the present, they can only make their voices heard within the context which currently exists. For the para-meters of public discourse in a constitutional state can only be legit-imately transformed from within.

The Goal and the Addressees

As citizens of this country, present-day Germans seek a symbolic expression for their political self-understanding which is essentially characterized by the historical reference to Auschwitz. They thereby wish to reaffirm the identity of a nation committed to civil rights in a version appropriate to our history. This declarative meaning of the memorial alone does not permit a single answer to the question con-cerning for what and for whom the memorial is intended, or con-cerning its location or appearance. The purpose of this memorial cannot be to elevate the Holocaust to the "founding myth of the Federal Republic."

To be sure, the German *Kulturnation* forged a bond with univer-salistic constitutional principles anchored in convictions only after and *through* Auschwitz, through the long-delayed public reflection on the final, previously unimaginable stage in the systematic exclu-sion and expulsion of Jews and communists, foreigners, the weak, those who thought and lived differently – that is, of all those offi-cially stigmatized as "internal enemies" – a process which was plain to see from the first days of the Nazi regime. This sad fact is not an "obsession" but a fact. It should not lead us to fixate on the loading dock of Auschwitz in a way that blocks cultural memory and pre-vents it from reaching back beyond the Nazi period. Strauss and Dregger consistently fed this suspicion with the slogan that the 1,000-year history of the Reich should not be reduced to the short 12-year history of the "1,000-year Reich."

On the occasion of the Walser debate, Karl-Heinz Bohrer recently made a forceful attempt to illuminate this murky sentiment with a good argument (in the *Neue Zürcher Zeitung*, December 12–13, 1998): "Remembrance only occurs when many things are remem-bered." No one would dispute this. But the historical reference to Auschwitz should not and cannot fix the citizens' gaze (and here we are only talking about their political self-understanding, not about historical research!) on the "one thing" that blinds them to everything else. Any halfway reasonable appropriation of tradition presupposes a multiplicity of perspectives on history. In the identity-forming process of coming to terms with the complexity of history, the commemoration of Auschwitz performs a kind of monitoring function that demands that traditions be tested, because after Auschwitz national self-confidence can only be derived from the better traditions of our history which we no longer simply take for granted but appropriate in a critical fashion.

Although the public reinforcement of this kind of self-confidence involves the desire for stability, current generations can claim such irrevocability only for themselves. They cannot bind future generations – nor should they wish to. Of course, the act of self-reassurance symbolically embodied in the memorial, which is not coincidentally supposed to mark the beginning of the Berlin Republic, is directed to the Germans of the future. The goal of the memorial is to challenge future generations to take a stand, to take a stance on what the memorial expresses, what Auschwitz meant for German identity a half century after the event. They should not shirk this challenge, whatever form the response takes, through avoidance or indifference. In this way, the memorial (*Denkmal*) – the word "*Denkmal*," by the way, acquired the narrower meaning of "monument" only in the seventeenth century – becomes an admonition (*Mahnmal*).

The Form of the Monument

The goal of the memorial explains why neither the authenticity of ruins or commemorative sites which document a past event, nor museum exhibits, collections or archives which are designed to inform, can serve as substitutes for a memorial. Only a memorial can attest to the will and the message of its sponsors. And only an uncompromising form of art can provide it with an appropriate language. Anyone who wants something more comfortable or more discursive has not grasped the meaning and the point of the project. The pointing finger of museum or heritage-site pedagogy is something different from the pointing finger of St John the Baptist on the altarpiece of Matthias Grünewald.[6]

Of course, a radically secularized politics can no longer rely on religious references. In late modernity there is no longer any universally shared context in which traditional symbols and rituals can produce collective allegiances that render justification superfluous. Nowadays the effect of a memorial that is not an aesthetic failure is always also nourished by the fluctuating reservoir of reasons that led to its erection. On the other hand, the cultural memory of a nation, which must not be confused with private memory, cannot propagate itself in the discursive medium of historiography, literature, and pedagogy alone. It remains dependent on symbolic representation and ritualization, although the forms and ideas which inspire such a project must be stripped of any appearance of naturalness in the acid bath of relentless public discourse.

It is difficult, perhaps impossible, to represent the collapse of civilization in the medium of art. And yet, for the act that here seeks symbolic expression, there is no better medium than that of the plastic arts, as the abstract, formal language of modern art, whose forbiddingly hermetic character still provides the best protection against embarrassing trivialization. Every step in the direction of concretization leads into the trap of false abstractions. For example, the general statement "thou shalt not kill" would only obscure the uncompromisingly specific meaning of the unthinkable, even if the injunction were repeated in Hebrew and spelled out in the various native languages of the murdered victims. I certainly could have imagined a different site and a different design from Serra and Eisenmann's stelae field – for example, Salomon Korn's proposal for a "yawning chasm" before the entrance to the parliament building in Berlin, which anyone entering or leaving the Bundestag would have to cross. However, as an echo of the crack in the façade of the Jewish Community Center in Frankfurt, that would have represented a borrowing.

Aesthetic discourses, in any event, cannot be conducted with the expectation of finding a "single right answer." In view of this fact, it will have to suffice that there is no obviously better alternative to the proposal on which the political discussion seems to be converging. Only the choice of a Jewish architect from the United States, though not the selection of the winning design, might provoke a slight suspicion that the jury tacitly shirked the responsibility which in this case must be borne by Germans alone. Never mind. If the memorial is to prompt future generations to take a stand, then it should be impossible to overlook, though it should not achieve this conspicuousness through monumentality. By "monumentalism" here, I mean the petrifying impression created by a triumphalist *Herrschaftsarchitektur*. In any case, the discreet pathos of the negative which characterizes the "Eisenmann II" design undercuts this objection. The vaguely troubling wave of silently arrayed, starkly looming pillars may isolate the visitors; but if I am right, it will not fill them with awe in the manner of monumental art.

The Challenge

Finally, we must take seriously the recently expressed fear of György Konrád that popular resentment, reacting to this stark challenge, might fall back on the Jews themselves rather than on the well-meaning sponsors. However seriously this warning should be taken, it is nevertheless of the same kind as the other, more trivial concerns voiced by those who, as petty as they are clever, anticipate vandalism by skinheads and their ilk. Their faintheartedness amounts to resignation in the face of the very mentality which the monument opposes. If we really want such a memorial, then it must also be as a barometer for the sentiments we wish to overcome – otherwise we betray the project itself. For as long as the integrity of the memorial cannot be assured without a massive, round-the-clock police presence, our country has not yet achieved the kind of ambivalent normality that is here, for the time being, the only kind possible.

On the other hand, we need to be clear about the kind of challenge which the monument represents. "One cannot erect a monument to one's own shame": Hermann Lübbe, Rudolf Augstein, and Martin Walser articulate a feeling that many share.[7] They speak within a tradition of the cult of sacrifice which, still during my own youth, was devoted to the image of the heroic dead, of the supposedly voluntary sacrifice for the "higher" good of the collective. The Enlightenment had good reasons for wanting to abolish sacrifice. The age of European nationalism was literally framed by thousands of war memorials, whose purpose was to commemorate in a triumphalist manner those who sacrificed themselves for the self-affirming nation. If today's descendants of the perpetrators of a uniquely monstrous act are to erect a memorial to the alien and the expelled, to the passive victims, then this triumphalist perspective has to change.

The issue at stake remains the self-understanding of the Germans. But the planned memorial will no longer direct the visitor's reverent gaze to the nation's dead, as the Vietnam Memorial in Washington still does, though no longer in a triumphalist way. The public's gaze must now be directed to the victims, who were turned into aliens by the actions and the omissions of our own parents and grandparents, repudiated as enemies, humiliated as subhumans, and tormented and annihilated as humans who were supposed to be stripped of their humanity. Moreover, this self-critical transgression is demanded of a nation with a bad conscience concerning its own war dead, whose memory has been more or less privatized out of an understandable embarrassment. The guilt of the survivors toward their fallen brothers remains to this day an important but unspoken motif in the most pertinent public debates concerning self-understanding in the Federal Republic.

The demand, therefore, is to apply moral viewpoints, which have long since been legally anchored in norms of civic equality within Western societies, in a non-selective way, without regard to belonging or membership. The Holocaust demands that Germans perform a spatial and temporal extension of the moral responsibility of democratic civil society that is incompatible with traditional national death cults. Is this already an expression of a "negative nationalism," as many people seem to think?

Helmut Dubiel and Bernd Giesen (neither of whom happens to be a historian) have cited examples from other nations to document the general trend toward a de-centered collective self-understanding that includes the injured others. In Spain, South Africa, and the United States, for example, controversies over the dark side of colonial history are being conducted which show similarities to our own "Historians' Debate," in structure if not in content. The period of collaboration is finally catching up with the French, Italians, Dutch, and Swedes. For all of them, it holds that "now one's own national past no longer [provides] the material for a positive reaffirmation of the *status quo*. Rather, it becomes a contrastive foil for understanding the present. Public memory of the national past is now assigned the task of breaking the mythic repetition-compulsion of a history burdened with guilt and injustice."[8] With this change in collective self-understanding, the universalism of the constitutional state catches up with the particularism of its sibling, national consciousness, by restructuring it from within, so to speak. In this way, nations also begin to feel the impact of the postnational constellation.

The Open Question: For Whom?

The moral universalism of equal respect for everybody cannot always be harmonized with the ethical particularism of the historical points of references in which the citizens of a nation recognize each other. The tension between a perpetrator- and a victim-centered understanding also erupts in the controversy over whether the planned memorial should be dedicated to "the murdered Jews" or to all victim groups. Reinhart Koselleck and Christian Meier have repeatedly drawn attention to the universalistic intuition that we should resist "establishing hierarchies among different groups of victims." In commemorating the victims, we must not once again sort them according to the criteria by which they were selected by their tormentors and subjected to different grades of suffering. Whereas the dedication of the Neue Wache to the "victims of war and dictatorship" involved an intolerable abstraction that jumbled together victims and perpetrators,[9] the exclusive reference to the murdered Jews now reflects a particularism that ignores the victims of other groups, at least at the same site. Implicitly at least, this particularization seems to represent an injustice to the Sinti and Roma, the political prisoners, the mentally handicapped, the homosexuals, the Jehovah's Witnesses, and the deserters, which demands some redress. As a result, the mayor of Berlin, Eberhard Diepgen, somewhat tactlessly fears the emergence of a "victim's mile," though this casually cynical remark highlights the endlessly complicated problems generated by justified claims to equal treatment.

Many people find the universalistic argument convincing. Even a Hermann Cohen[10] would have agreed with it. Salomon Korn, Mischa Brumlik, and many Jews here in Germany share Koselleck's and Meier's view. Nevertheless, we cannot overlook the fact which explains why for us today "Auschwitz" is interwoven in such an overwhelming way with the Holocaust of the European Jews. The moral intuition to which universalists rightly appeal intersects with another, if you will, ethical intuition, which refers to our own collectivity. Were we to ignore the special relevance of the Jews for the social and cultural life of Germany, the historically fraught, quite specific proximity and distance of both of these unequal poles, wouldn't we once again be guilty of a false abstraction?

A differential treatment of victims who all ultimately suffered the same fate cannot be morally justified. But another factor has to be added to the moral scales. The various grades of horror that the perpetrators and their accomplices, the sympathizers and those who looked on impassively, visited upon Jews and non-Jews reflect a spectrum of motives whose extreme, as Saul Friedländer has remarked, was the "redemptive anti-Semitism" of the Germans and their elites. Without the special relevance which the Jews had in the eyes of their German fellow-citizens, for better or for worse, the atrocity and the support for it would ultimately have lacked any motive. A good illustration of this is the cultural interaction between Jews and Germans since the opening of the ghettos. The German-Jewish symbiosis which, in Scholem's words, was from the beginning asymmetrical and tension-laden, but also productive and founded on spiritual affinities, had a darker side. Among the academically trained strata and the intellectuals in particular (who in the Weimar period still referred to themselves as "the learned" – *die Geistigen*), cultural anti-Semitism had become ingrained. Without this mentality, it would be impossible to explain either the scandalous willingness of the educated bourgeoisie to accommodate themselves or the moral corruption of previously sustaining traditions.

The intuition concerning the special social and cultural significance of the Jews for us Germans must not neutralize the unconditional moral obligation to show equal respect in commemorating all victims. The "deed-" and "perpetrator-centered" meaning of the memorial should not overshadow the "victim-centered" meaning of remembrance as such. Otherwise, by failing to show appropriate respect for that special relevance, we would abstract from a particularly fateful mentality of segregation and exclusion which should be incorporated into the critical self-attributions of cultural memory. For reasons of honesty toward ourselves, therefore, it would be desirable that the difference in relevance should find expression in a non-exclusive dedication of the memorial.

I am not sure whether "Auschwitz Memorial" can express both things. The memorial itself does not have any name other than that of the extermination camp engraved in one place. Nevertheless, it needs a name for administrative purposes, for the street signs, and above all in public consciousness. The collective name "Auschwitz" which first gained currency is now used almost synonymously with the expression "Holocaust" which was adopted later. But in fact, it encompasses more than the fate of the Jews alone. As *pars pro toto* it signifies the complex enterprise of destruction as a whole.

Part III

Public Representation and Cultural Memory

The controversy over the Berlin memorial poses the fundamental question of how the commemoration of identity-forming events of recent history can today still find appropriate symbolic representation in the cultural memory of citizens. I addressed this question on December 9, 1998, at the University of Dresden, on the occasion of a symposium organized by the Research Group on "Institutionality and Historicity." The text of the lecture appeared in Gert Melville, ed., *Institutionalität und Symbolisierung* (Cologne: Böhlau, 2001), pp. 53–68.

5

Symbolic Expression and Ritual Behavior: Ernst Cassirer and Arnold Gehlen Revisited

I

Certain kinds of institution, such as dynastic clans and banking houses, empires and urban communes, churches, academies, and business firms, cannot be fully explained in functional terms, that is, in terms of their organizational structure. Such institutions also secure collective bonds and loyalties by means of symbolic modes of expression and ceremonial practices. In comparison with everyday, rationally comprehensible forms of behavioral coordination and control, these appellative and ritualistic forms preserve a non-discursive affective and imaginary core. We can distinguish such "strong" institutions – which have, however, become progressively weaker in modern times – from mere organizations by their appearance of "naturalness." Both at the cognitive level of communicated contents and at the performative level of behavioral patterns, they exhibit a surplus of symbolization. In many cases, of course, this surplus has dwindled to little more than the corporate logo on a company's letterhead, the triumphal architecture of a brash banking house, modern art hanging in the boardroom, or the annual company outing. Strong institutions give rise to self-referential traditions and practices that fulfill two primary functions. Toward the outside, they make possible the manifest representation of a self-defined role that is nevertheless intended to gain general recognition; in other words, they facilitate a publicly effective interpretation of the institution's accomplishments and the symbolic representation of its importance. Toward the inside, these traditions and practices give expression to an intersubjectively shared and normatively binding self-understanding for colleagues or members. This is why we speak of something like the "collective identity" of a citizen body, a congregation or a workforce.

How do phenomena such as these fit into the theoretical landscape of contemporary sociology? Rational choice theory and systems theory would perhaps inquire into the latent functions of such marginal phenomena, which they regard as residues of a practice originally founded on different reasons. By contrast, the classical theory of social action originating in Weber and Parsons explains behavioral stabilization and social order in terms of institutionalization. However, these theories also tend to downplay symbolic aspects, because they understand institutionalization in terms of the interplay of ideas and interests that can also be stabilized without the aid of ceremonial practices. Emile Durkheim's sociology of religion comes closest to explaining these kinds of phenomena. But what remains of the sacred origins of the power of social integration after the communicative dissolution of myth and magic, religion and ritual? Durkheim himself seems to emphasize the continuities when he asks, for example, whether there is any essential difference between a congregation of the faithful celebrating the Stations of the Cross and an association of citizens recollecting the founding of their political constitution or some other extraordinary event in their national history.

The affirmative answer which Durkheim still proposed at the beginning of the twentieth century is no longer so easy for us to accept at the end of the twentieth century, at any rate, not for us citizens of the German Federal Republic. Think of our hollow National Holiday, our garbled national anthem, and the relatively weak appeal of the red, black, and gold of our flag, of representative sites like the Bundeshaus or the Reichstag and of dates like July 20 or November 9.[1] In any case, the Federal Republic can scarcely be said to owe its amazing integrative power to its generally lacklustre symbolic self-representation. But we should also not be satisfied with the easy answer which points to the faded glory of the ceremonies and forms of expression by which the state publicly represents itself.

Apparently, even the Federal Republic still needs sites like the Neue Wache[2] and the rituals of state visits and public commemorations. In the context of state symbolism, the controversial project of a memorial for the murdered European Jews is revealing. The long and bitter controversy over the project, which was conducted with great seriousness and in full public view, shows what has changed since the routine war memorials of the nineteenth and early twentieth centuries – and why. What has changed is clear. The traditional forms of national collective memory initiated by the authorities and practiced by the population have been drawn into the current of reflection. As decision-making processes become increasingly discursive and pluralistic, symbols and ceremonies lose their quasi-natural character as something unconscious, inevitable, and unquestionably binding. Whatever "resolution" to the controversy ultimately emerges from the public political debate, everyone will be aware that the outcome could have been different. This will invest any future symbolic practice with an awareness of contingency, notwithstanding all routinization and trivialization, so that still later generations will also feel called upon to recall and, if necessary, to revise the reasons used to justify it.

Of course, this kind of reflexivity, which contrasts with the visible embodiment and the customary presentation of an event of existential significance, can also be explained in terms of the large-scale change in consciousness which is part of the process of social and political modernization. But, as our example shows, there is also a specific, moral-cognitive reason for the permanent reflection which refuses to leave the ethical-political self-understanding of *our* political community unexamined.

When the German descendants of the perpetrators erect a memorial to Jewish victims, the ethnocentric perspective which previously informed a nation's self-referential confirmation of its historical legacy can no longer be maintained. The focus of the culture of war memorials on the at once painful and commendable fate of the nation's war dead must now be expanded to include those victims who where transformed into aliens by the actions and omissions of our own parents and grandparents, and then expelled, humiliated, and annihilated. This moment of self-critical transcending of boundaries makes it difficult for a collective which seeks confirmation of a history defined within national boundaries to find a set form for such a practice. It is also what spurs on the ambivalent call for "normality." When Rudolf Augstein laments (in the last but one issue of *Der Spiegel*) that "Now, in the center of the recently recovered capital of

Berlin, a monument is supposed to be erected to remind us of our enduring shame," he is giving vent to the exasperation of the German particularism which shies away from the embarrassing scrutiny of others and the universalistic demand for a form of inclusion that transcends borders. Herman Lübbe says openly what Martin Walser thinks: "One can't erect a monument to one's own shame." In this respect all three are typical representatives of their generation.

I wonder whether this example may not point to a more general problem. The universalistic core of the constitutional state, and indeed the normative self-understanding of modernity as such, certainly do not render symbolic modes of expression or ritualistic forms of representation of collective identity obsolete. But the latter do appear to have lost their power to generate normative validity claims and to impose them by symbolic force alone, that is, unquestioningly. Can one still assert that the symbolic embodiment and ritualistic representation of the guiding ideas of political institutions which draw their legitimation from the heritage of rational natural law are still oriented to the "creation" of normative bonds and the "imposition" of normative validity claims? Is the persuasive power of expectations of norm-conforming behavior still rooted in representational acts which command emotions and take possession of minds? Or does the constitutional state ultimately depend on the presumptive acceptability of good reasons which has been institutionalized in the form of discursive procedures? Perhaps strong institutionalism is more tailored to the self-representations of late-totalitarian forms of government than to the symbolic achievements of the constitutional state. I look forward eagerly to answers to the question of whether a "strong" institution with a symbolic dimension can survive in the televised culture of the late twentieth century in the manner of the *mos majorum* of the Romans.

Here I must limit myself to a few remarks on the philosophical background of an approach to the theory of institutions that can be traced back to Hegel. For it was not the Kantian Durkheim but rather the Kant critic Hegel who first expressed fear concerning the destabilizing implications of moral universalism and sought to compensate for it through a critique of morality founded on the concept of "ethical life" [*Sittlichkeit*].

II

Hegel grounds his strong institutionalism in a critique of the supposed hostility to life of the "abstractness" of a purely formal "moral point of view" that is exclusively oriented to the universalization of interests and finds expression in Kant's categorical imperative. In the relevant paragraphs of the *Philosophy of Right* (§§105–56), Hegel shows that a universalistic ethics of duty, in contrast to an Aristotelian ethics of the good or a Humean ethics of sentiment, hangs in the air, so to speak. Above all, Hegel criticizes the inordinate demands for abstraction implied by Kant's ethics of duty. In the first place, it abstracts from the actual motives or inclinations of moral actors. Ethical commands do not necessarily harmonize either with personal preferences or with need-dispositions and value-orientations formed in the process of socialization. Second, Kantian ethics pays just as little attention to the problem of the foreseeability of complex consequences of actions for which actors may be held accountable. In indeterminate situations, good intentions often lead to bad outcomes. Kant overburdens not only the motivations, but also the cognitive capacities, of individuals. Finally, there is the problem of the application of general norms to particular cases which becomes especially pressing when norms which appear to be equally appropriate to a particular situation conflict with each other.

Hegel's arguments may be understood as asserting that "abstract morality" demands too high a motivational and cognitive effort from individuals. These deficits must be made good at the institutional level. What subjective spirit [*subjektiver Geist*] cannot accomplish must be compensated for by objective spirit [*objektiver Geist*]. The latter is embodied in intelligent "laws and institutions" which give the ethical "a fixed *content*." Hegel ascribes an "existence . . . exalted above subjective opinions and preferences" (§144) to objective ethical life. In the major institutions of society and the state, he identifies an existing reason which reaches beyond the limited horizons of the minds of individual subjects [*subjektiver Geist*]. For institutions coordinate ideas with interests and functions. They bring the justifying ideas of ethical and religious legitimations into harmony with the interests of individual members, on the one hand, and the functional imperatives of a differentiated society, on the other. This tension-laden integration explains why "the objective-ethical, which takes the place of the abstract good," relieves the good will and the cognitive faculties of overburdened individuals by assigning them clearly defined concrete duties: "In an ethical community, it is easy to say *what* someone must do and *what* the duties are which he has to fulfill in order to be virtuous. He must simply do what is prescribed, expressly stated, and known to him within his situation" (§150).

Hegel already describes institutions in which the "spirit of a people" is embodied in a similar way to Gehlen a century later. As a "second nature" (§151), institutions should "*not* be regarded as *something made*" (§273), but rather as "the divine and enduring" which has become independent of the goals and intentions of subjects. Furthermore, institutions which embody general interests depend on public representation. Hegel does not apply the customary political understanding of "representation" as implying a representative assembly even to parliaments; rather, here too he falls back on the expressive relation between essence and appearance: "Thus, representation no longer means the *replacement* of one individual *by another*; on the contrary, the interest itself is *actually present* in its representative" (§311). Finally, the substantial ethical life of institutions claims a superior authority in relation to the mere opinions of individual moral persons. The inverted morality of a deluded subject who opposes the objectively existing good by appealing to his "merely independent will" is the worst form of hypocrisy.

In contrast with Gehlen, however, Hegel insists on the condition that the self-conscious or rational subject does not have to acknowledge anything that he cannot accept as justified by his own lights. The modern state has "enormous strength and depth because it allows the principle of subjectivity to attain fulfillment in the *self-sufficient extreme* of personal particularity, while at the same time *bringing it back to substantial unity* and so preserving this unity in the principle of subjectivity itself" (§260). For this reason, Hegel subordinates subjective spirit to objective ethical life only with the proviso that the institutions must themselves assume a rational [*vernünftig*] form, in accordance with the principle of realizing equal freedoms for all. However, the judgment concerning whether and to what extent the existing institutions are rational may not be left to the active citizens themselves, but must instead be answered from the speculative standpoint of the philosopher. For the extent to which the institutions of civil society and the state are adequate to their concept can only be revealed to mind [*Geist*] which has reached the level of absolute knowledge beyond the sphere of objective spirit. Hence the privileged insight of the philosopher can never have practical consequences. His retrospective insight always comes too late for action.

So much for Hegel. But what becomes of the objective "good" when philosophy no longer trusts itself to plead for the rationality of the real – or at least to affirm that the real will become rational? What becomes of Hegel's institutionalism after Hegel? What becomes of an ethical life that retains its substantiality but forfeits its relation to reason? We can certainly describe the "spirit" of institutions, the spirit of the Roman tradition, of medieval cloisters, of courtly literature, of the welfare state or parliamentarianism. But we lack the standards by which we could judge whether these forms of spirit are rational. We scarcely know any longer what the question of the rationality of institutions beyond their mere stability is supposed to mean. The thread of objective idealism snapped in the course of the nineteenth century. The heightened consciousness of contingency in the historical sciences and the Darwinian principle of randomness governing natural evolution have driven speculative reason out of nature and history. Nevertheless, the concepts of objective spirit, ethical life, and institutions have all outlived the Hegelian system. After the unifying bond of reason was ruptured, Hegel's conception of ethical life disintegrated into the elements from which he originally constructed it: language, work, and interaction.

Already during his Jena period, in his assault on the mentalistic oppositions of mind and body and subject and object, Hegel had introduced *third* categories which are characterized by the fact that they anticipated the splitting of objective spirit into interiority and externality: non-material meanings find expression in the symbolic medium of *language*, subjective experiences in the expressive gestures of the *living body*, the intelligent intention of the *actor* in the movements of the working body, the self-consciousness of the person in interpersonal relations between actors, and the *spirit of a people* in practices, institutions, and customs: "The spirit of a people must forever become *accomplishment* [*Werk*]."[3] The conception of ethical life rests on the insight that the human mind [*der menschliche Geist*] is not merely subjective but also has both a constructive and a social character, because it can only exist in the symbolic objectifications of a second nature. This fundamental anti-Cartesian insight of Hegel's lives on in philosophical anthropology, no less than in pragmatism and historicism. The human mind encounters itself only indirectly, through symbolically mediated relations to the world; it does not exist "in the head" but in the totality of publicly accessible and inter-subjectively comprehensible symbolic expressions and practices.

In the 1920s and 1930s, philosophical anthropology assimilated this foundational idea after its own fashion, namely, on the non-idealistic, post-Hegelian premise of the priority of nature and natural history to humankind (also in an ontological sense). Ernst Cassirer, Helmut Plessner, and Arnold Gehlen sought to explain the symbolic construction of a second nature by drawing on Max Scheler's account of the initial conditions of an organically deficient human being which has broken its ties with species-specific environments and is characterized by "openness to the world." However, in contrast with Scheler, they rejected any recourse to the "principle" of a negating spirit that intervenes like a metaphysical lightning-bolt in the organic life of animals in order to compensate for the organic deficiencies of human beings through intellectual intuition and propositional atti-tudes toward the world of facts. Cassirer, Plessner, and Gehlen focus instead on the symbolic media of an at once constructive and indi-rect, but increasingly complex, relation of the knowing and acting subject to the world and to itself. Cassirer investigated the symbolic forms of world disclosure, Plessner expressive bodily behavior, and Gehlen both instrumental and ritualistic interactions with a world fraught with danger.

A comparison between the theories of Cassirer and Gehlen can show us that how we understand symbolic expression and ritualistic behavior also determines how we answer the broader question of what relation, if any, exists between institutionality and symboliza-tion, on the one hand, and rationality, on the other. The question is how practices and modes of representation within contemporary institutions shape people's minds; specifically, whether symbolic pre-sentations and their normative fictions *create* institutional bonds or whether they merely reinforce normative validity claims grounded in some other way – that is, whether they merely contribute to the process by which rationally acquired insights become rooted in the motives and attitudes of participants. Do symbolic practices still remain the ultimate source of non-rationalizable bonds and loyalties after the Enlightenment, or do they merely invest a normativity of an essentially discursive kind whose origins lie elsewhere with an aura popular appeal? Gehlen pursues the first of these paths, Cassirer the second.

III

Like Scheler and philosophical anthropology in general, Cassirer determines the "special status" of human beings, that is, the specificity of their socio-cultural form of life, by comparison with animal life forms. He too draws on the model of species-specific environments developed in the biological-behavioral sciences by Johannes von Uexküll. According to this model, there is a correlation between animal organisms and their environments for a specific range of sensory stimuli and a specific set of behavioral dispositions, namely, instinctively regulated bodily movements triggered by highly selective stimuli. In contrast to this isomorphic relation between organism and environment, the human being's relation to the world is indirect because symbolic forms intervene as connecting links between the perceptual system and the motor functions:

> No longer in a merely physical universe, man lives in a symbolic universe. Language, myth, art, and religion are parts of this universe. They are the varied threads which weave the symbolic net, the tangled web of human existence. . . . No longer can man confront reality immediately. . . . Physical reality seems to recede in proportion as man's symbolic activity advances. . . . He has so enveloped himself in linguistic forms, in artistic images, in mythical symbols, or religious rites that he cannot see or know anything except by the interposition of this artificial medium.[4]

The contrast between human beings' openness to the world and animals' dependency on specific environments, which for Scheler is grounded in the objectifying attitude toward the world of facts, acquires a different emphasis in Cassirer. For the human observer, species-specific environments certainly constitute only selective excerpts from the larger universe he surveys; but what appears to him as an objective world turns out to be a symbolic construction that is dependent on the observer's own use of language. Human beings find themselves in symbolic worlds which exhibit less selectivity, but also, in a certain sense, greater fallibility, than animal environments. For symbolic worlds are not determined by objective correlations between organic equipment and salient features of the environment, but result from the constructive coping with surprising and frustrating experiences.

Cassirer undertakes a semiotic transformation of Kantian epistemology, transferring the spontaneity of world-constitution from the transcendental subject to various "languages": the language of everyday life, of myth, of art, of religion, of science, and so on. The various symbolic "worlds" which we simultaneously inhabit reflect as many views of the world as forms of practical interaction with the world: rites, everyday practices, arts, cults, procedures and institutions, handicrafts, aesthetic and scientific techniques, and so on. In this very broad conception of "symbolic forms," the specific distinction that is of interest in the present context seems to disappear in a continuum. On the one side stand linguistic, propositionally structured, and hence rational, forms of representation and action with explicit meaning contents; on the other, the non-discursive, pre- or extra-linguistic, ritualized, imagistic modes of expression or styles, whose performative or pre-predicative meaning-contents await, as it were, explication in the linguistic medium. In Cassirer's view, both the rational and the irrational aspects interpenetrate in the process of symbolization.[5]

As a member of the Warburg Circle, Cassirer took the genesis of names of gods and goddesses as a basis for investigating the original acts of symbolization which transform fleeting sensory stimuli into semantic meaning, in such a way that affected subjects can store their impressions in memory in a retrievable, and hence readily accessible, form. By founding an invariant set of meanings, such acts provide a medium for thoughts that transcends the stream of experience. Cassirer understands this process of symbolic sublimation as a response to the ambivalence of exciting and intense experiences. Dramatically intense experiences – the hill offering a life-saving refuge for someone being pursued, water in the oasis that prevents one from dying of thirst, bolts of lightning, wild animals, and, in general, situations that simultaneously attract and repulse – all of these can condense into mythic or cultic images, and can thereby become semanticized, fixed in the form of a god's name, recollected, spellbound, and thereby mastered. The affective tension is both diverted and stabilized by the transformation of sensory impressions into symbolic expressions. Yet the subject would remain trapped in its world of images if the symbolizing process were exhausted by the semanticization of particular intense experiences.

The *spellbinding* [*bannend*] tendency toward the formal congealing of isolated impressions into a symbolic image is complemented by the *concept-forming* tendency toward generalization and differentiation. Symbolic "worlds," such as those of myth and everyday communication, are the result of the interplay of countervailing processes. They arise *simultaneously* from the production of images pregnant with meaning and the logical disclosure of a coherent, categorically articulated domain of experience. The mythic image serves as a placeholder for "the mute fullness of Being" which finds an outlet in a "linguistically comprehensible structure" in statements. Two processes of meaning-creation are interconnected in the procedure of symbolization: one tends toward *expression*, the other toward *concept-formation*. These tendencies by no means figure equally in the various symbolic forms. Where the spellbinding tendency crystallizes sensory impressions into images, the expressive function remains dominant, as in the case of myth; where the concept-forming tendency toward articulation and abstraction prevails, the statement-making function wins out, as in science; and where both tendencies are in equilibrium, the representational function comes to the fore, as in everyday experience or, in a different manner, in art.

These elective affinities suggest the possibility of arraying the symbolic functions of sensuous "expression," graphic "representation," and pure "propositional meaning" on a scale of progressive decontextualization and objectification. This tendency toward abstraction can also be observed within a single symbolic world. At the level of iconoclastic monotheistic religions, even the mythic form of thought turns against its own principle of imagistic condensation. On the other hand, the cults and the languages of prayer of these major religions can never entirely liberate themselves from their mythic origins; otherwise they would destroy their distinctive symbolic form and forfeit their sacred character. Since no symbolic form loses its distinctive character in favor of higher symbolic forms, we live simultaneously in different, co-original symbolic worlds. At the same time, however, the different symbolic orders, as well as each of them internally, exhibit different degrees of complexity in accordance with which the distance, the freedom, and the reflexivity of the knowing and acting subjects themselves simultaneously vary.

In this sense, the function of conferring symbolic form has an inherent normative component. As human beings master the forces of nature that assail them through symbols, they gain a measure of distance from the immediate pressure of nature. To be sure, the price they pay for this liberation is the self-imposed dependence on a semanticized nature, which returns in the magical power of mythical images. But the break with the first nature continues within this second, symbolically generated nature, namely, with the conceptual tendency toward the construction and categorical articulation of symbolic *worlds*. As civilization advances, humanity entangles itself in an ever-denser web of symbolic mediations, thereby freeing itself from the contingencies of a nature with which it enters into contact in increasingly indirect ways. This dynamic of the advance of civilization is simultaneously a dynamic of the civilizing process: "The most basic feature of human existence seems to be that human beings do not simply dissolve in the wealth of external impressions, but that they hold this wealth in check by imposing a determinate form on it which ultimately proceeds from within, from the thinking, feeling, willing subject."[6] The symbolizing animal finds itself entangled in processes of development for which growing individual and, ultimately, political freedoms provide the compass as its life processes become progressively symbolically mediated. Of course, a compass can only give the direction; it cannot ensure that the right path will be chosen or that it will be consistently pursued.

Cassirer always remained true to the forbidding, humanist pathos of Kant's morality of reason. However, he never wrote a philosophical ethics because he thought that the liberating and civilizing tendencies of an indirect relation to the world were inscribed in the processes of symbolization themselves. He constructed a continuum between imagistic expression and concept through the unity of symbolic form-giving in the manifold of symbolic forms of expression, thereby securing for each form of spirit its own rationality. Cassirer did not drive a wedge between rationality and normativity, and he did not reserve rationality for linguistic communication, purposive-rational action, and scientific discourse in order to locate the source of normative validity in mythic storytelling, ritualistic practice, or art. There is no contradiction between the persuasive force of discursively justified norms and the binding power of forms of ritualistic behavior. The relationship is a complementary one.

One of Cassirer's own public appearances can serve as an illustration of this point. I have in mind an address he delivered on August 11, 1928 as one of the few prominent defenders of the Weimar

Republic on the tenth anniversary of its constitution. Clearly, the arguments he presented on the occasion of the "constitutional cele-bration" organized by the Free State of Hamburg acquired a differ-ent status from what they had earlier in the context of an academic lecture. But did they thereby become merely the rhetorical expres-sion of a public institution's ceremonial self-representation? Both the institutional framework provided by the Hamburg citizenry and the public authority of its organizers were able to lend the speaker's argu-ments greater public impact and a certain political weight. But was the content of the speech itself thereby ceremonialized or diverted into the expression of an *idée directrice*? The arguments first had to speak for themselves if they were to have a rhetorical impact. For on this occasion Cassirer attempted to win over a presumably nationalist-conservative, and certainly anti-Western, public for the Weimar Republic through the sole force of his arguments and to convince them "that the idea of the republican constitution is by no means foreign to German intellectual history, let alone an alien intruder."[7]

Even in periods and under conditions when republican institutions are secure, such self-affirming ceremonies – think of the celebrations of the bicentennial of the American Constitution in Philadelphia in 1976 – remain contingent on recollecting the good reasons which originally moved a constitutional convention to found a political community on the basis of equal civil rights for all. For later gener-ations, too, who feel obliged to uphold the project of realizing rights that were only selectively realized in the past, the necessary affective bond must have a rational kernel if it is not to atrophy completely. In these important cases for modern social conditions, the normative validity claim of the institution is so closely bound up with discur-sive justifications that a ceremony serves rather to represent reasons in graphic form than the converse, namely, to offer reasons that promote the self-representation of public institutions.

IV

Arnold Gehlen takes a different view. He cannot detect the slightest trace of reason in the distinctive unconditional mode of obligation of binding norms, only the promise of stability offered by the symbolic

power of institutions and powerful ideas. The latter can impose
duties on their addressees only so long as they are shielded from criticism, public reflection, and justification.

This conception follows from an anthropology that proceeds in
turn from the "openness to the world" of humanity and understands
the construction of cultural forms of life as compensating for the deficient functional adaptation of a species that is indeterminate and
incomplete from a biological point of view. Referring to George
Herbert Mead's mechanism of role-taking and perspective-taking,
Gehlen too emphasizes the indirect relation to the world of a creature who can only relate to itself via a relation to something other
and objective. But unlike Cassirer, Mead, and Plessner, Gehlen does
not choose symbolic mediation – whether in the form of the semanticization of sense impressions, symbolic interaction, or bodily expression – as a third, non-mentalistic category that is neutral between
body and mind. Action takes the place of symbolization. The mor-
phologically ill-adapted human animal can ward off the high risks of
a natural environment that overwhelms him with diffuse stimuli only
by refashioning dangerous contingencies into challenges for an intelligent and success-oriented form of action and by constructing an
objective world of perceptible and manipulable objects and events
geared to solving such practical problems.

The idea of disburdening through instrumental action is what
unites Gehlen's anthropology with the pragmatism of John Dewey.
But unlike Dewey, Gehlen is concerned not only with the risks of an
unpredictable external nature but in particular with the risks of an
unstable internal nature. The decoupling of the human motor functions from instinctual steering left behind a de-differentiated, shifting, and chronically over-active drive potential. The plasticity of the
drives and the variability of learned movements do indeed facilitate
imaginative exploration, curiosity-driven experimentation, and learning. But the non-specific oppressive drive-energies threaten the
objectivity of action, so that this very disburdening mechanism must
itself be disburdened of the "surplus of drives." The increasing complexity and objectification of work, tool use, and the rational domination of nature demand the deferral and disciplining of drives. This
is especially necessary for successful long-term social cooperation, for
"given human beings' world-openness and freedom from instinct,
nothing guarantees that collective action will actually occur . . . or
that it won't break down again tomorrow."[8]

All known societies have solved this problem through the normative stabilization of behavior, and the question concerning the origin
of normativity requires that the anthropological approach be
extended to include a theory of institutions. Institutions make "purposeless yet obligatory action" possible. Unless strong institutions
intervene to fill the need for regulation left by the absence of instinctual guidance, humans succumb to the pressure of their drifting drives
and fall into the "state of chronic ego-consciousness" and "the self-
satisfaction of subjectivity." Vico's "barbarism of reflection" is the main
inspiration for this dramatization, for here "reflection" means that the
space of imagination uncoupled from direct experience is flooded
with wish-fulfillment fantasies and closes itself off narcissistically from
the demands of realistic behavior. This deep-seated "degenerative"
tendency can only be blocked by normatively binding actions.

Like Hegel, Gehlen invokes strong institutions as a counterweight
to a hypertrophied subjectivity that no longer guarantees the stability of ethical behavior. But he tries to explain the phenomenon for
which Hegel developed the concept of objective spirit – "the independence which institutions acquire in relation to individuals" – on
a "more realistic level."[9] "Realistic" here means that we determine the
objective rationality of institutions without reference to the subjective reason of individuals. Hegel still insisted on the fact that each
individual person must retain an equal opportunity to develop his
freedom, individuality, and independence within ethical life as a
whole. For him, existing reason also consists in the fact that the state
makes possible the perfection "of personal particularity . . . to an
independent extreme." For Gehlen, the individual person is nothing
other than "an institution of one."[10] According to Hegel, no one need
acquiesce in a normative authority if he is not convinced of the
reasons for its legitimacy. Gehlen, by contrast, makes a clear separation between the objective rationality of institutions, on the one
hand, and the subjective irrationality of motives, on the other. Individuals must submerge themselves completely in their status and "let
themselves be consumed by existing institutions, [for] outside them
they cannot find a foothold."[11]

Gehlen makes several attempts to explain the peculiar normativity of "purposeless but obligatory action." In success-oriented, trial-
and-error, combinatory, and reconstructive modes of action, the actor
already encounters the external authority of "objective laws." Anyone
who invests his efforts in the production of objects, or identifies with

his tasks and develops corresponding work habits, subjects himself to the "veto of the things themselves." However, the cognitive compulsion experienced in "coping" – that is, intelligent grappling with reality – cannot explain the special binding force of social behavioral expectations. What we "ought" to do in contexts of social interaction obligates in a different way from the mute demands of nature to which we "must" submit in instrumental action.

In the next step, therefore, Gehlen falls back on the functional independence of habitual behavior in relation to the motives from which it originally arose. The imprecise formula of "the separation of motive and end" refers to patterns of behavior that are stabilized through an unintended purposiveness. They switch over into a "self-sufficient autarky." Niklas Luhmann developed this idea of the decoupling of organizations from the motives of their members into a systems theory that displaces persons entirely into the environments of social systems, thereby rendering the question of the origin of normativity moot. This inference reveals that the obligatory character of binding norms of action can no more be explained by reference to the functional rationality of institutions and organizations than by the rationality of the success-oriented action of individual agents.

Lacking a different, more inclusive conception of rationality, Gehlen can conceive of the imperative force of the ought which functions analogously to instinct only as an irrational bond which hides its own irrationality from itself. In order to explain this phenomenon, Gehlen must ultimately extend his anthropological approach to include a second type of behavior, that of ritualistic or "representational behavior." In this way he brings the symbols and practices from which such a spellbinding force seems to issue into view – for example, the animal images of early palaeolithic cave paintings and the related ritualistic practices. Not unlike Cassirer three decades earlier, Gehlen explains the symbolic representation and ritualistic imitation of scenes from the game hunts as an affect-stabilizing response to ambivalent emotions triggered by dangerous impressions and experiences. The symbolic imitation of the impressions in images and the ritualistic re-enactment of experiences in rhythmic bodily movements charge the cultic object with the at once fascinating and intimidating authority of an "intrinsic value," which confronts the actor like an external imperative: "To act from the begin-thus of things means allowing them to respond. . . . This stabilization of the external world was human beings' first great cultural act."[12] Through ritualistic action, we enter "into the sphere of normed behavior without changing objects."[13] In ritual, our behavior is normed through the symbolic force of a tabooed counterpart, no longer through objects which we compel to yield informative answers through experimentation.

Because all normative stabilization of behavior ultimately draws its sustenance from symbolic imitation, the major institutions also crystallize around the leading ideas into which these primitive cultic images have been sublimated. These *idées directrices* do not play a cognitive role, but mobilize affects and attitudes when they find a representative expression. They remain effective only as long as they are withdrawn from discursive thematization, and they decay together with the institutions in which they are embodied.[14] Unlike Cassirer, who locates the tension between expression and concept in the symbolic medium itself, Gehlen excludes the possibility of a rationalization of the quasi-natural kernel of institutions as represented in ritual. For Gehlen, the "overwhelming superiority of representation over the concept" consists in the fact that ritualistic action renders the imperatival "being-thus" of extraordinary things durable, whereas concepts merely express fleeting and revisable opinions.

Wherein lies the problem? Gehlen introduced the category of representational action as a way of explaining the sacred origins of the authority of binding norms of action. Given his premises, the explanation makes sense. But this genesis of the ought does not explain why all normative validity must remain tied to this origin. From the perspective of an immanent critique, the theory of drives – the assumption of burgeoning needs uncoupled from action – does not represent the limit, but the far too narrow basis of a theory of action that distorts our view of a process of cultural rationalization. For the latter unfolds in communicative action. The communicative dissolution of the normative contents of myths and rituals, of symbolic modes of expression and practices, certainly implies a transformation, but not the disintegration, of the grounds of the validity of "purposeless obligatory action."[15]

Symbolic forms of representation and ritualistic forms of expression occur in modern societies, and not only in residual forms. The example of the Berlin Holocaust memorial project already mentioned shows that the cultural memory of a nation is not only transmitted in the discursive media of education, literary traditions, and the pedagogy of museums and memorials; clearly it requires symbolic

representation and ritualization as well. On the other hand, prior to
the realization of a project of this sort, the forms and ideas that render
it so inspiring are also stripped of their last vestiges of naturalness in
the acid bath of relentless public discourse. Neither Hegel's ethical
life nor Gehlen's institutions is the appropriate concept for this.

Part IV

Europe in Transition

The issue of the future of the European Union is commanding greater attention under the pressure of the "enlargement crisis." The first of the two following lectures was delivered in February 1999 at St Gallen University and appeared in Peter Ulrich and Thomas Maak (eds.), *Die Wirtschaft in der Gesellschaft* (Bern: Haupt, 2000), pp. 151–72. The debate over the EU Constitution initiated by Joschka Fischer, and subsequently taken up by Chirac, Prodi, Rau, Schröder, and Jospin, prompted me to address the same issue – with an immediate political goal in mind – at the invitation of the Senate of the City of Hamburg and the Zeit-Stiftung on June 26, 2001 at the University of Hamburg. The talk was based on a text (published in abridged form in the June 28 issue of *Die Zeit*) that I had previously delivered in Paris, Rome, Madrid, and England.

6

Euroskepticism, Market Europe, or a Europe of (World) Citizens?

"The question which currently overshadows all others," we read in the introduction to a new book entitled *Global Dynamics and Local Environments*, "is whether the power of global capitalism to wreak ecological, social, and cultural havoc can be brought back under control beyond the level of the nation-state, that is, at the supranational and global levels."[1] No one disputes the power of markets for innovation and coordination. But markets only respond to messages coded in the language of prices. They are insensible to the externalities they produce in other domains. This gives the liberal sociologist Richard Münch reason to fear that we will be faced with the depletion of non-renewable natural resources, cultural alienation on a mass scale, and social eruptions, unless we succeed in setting political controls on markets that are, as it were, outrunning enfeebled and overburdened nation-states. Münch detects an "inflationary overextension" of economic modernization, which will lead to the "deflationary downward spiral" of an aggressive group particularism, even in the prosperous societies of the North.

Certainly, the call for an "ecological, social and cultural re-embedding of global capitalism" is something of a euphemism. States in advanced capitalist societies aggravated rather than defused the explosive ecological threats during the postwar period; and they built social security systems through social-welfare bureaucracies which did not exactly promote the individual autonomy of their clients. Yet, in the third quarter of the twentieth century, the welfare state largely succeeded in offsetting the undesirable social consequences of a highly productive economic system in Europe and the other OECD countries. For the first time, capitalism made possible the fulfillment, rather than the frustration, of the republican promise of the equal inclusion of all citizens. For constitutional democracy also guarantees equality before the law in the sense of citizens' equal opportunity to exercise their rights. John Rawls, the most influential contemporary theorist of political liberalism, speaks in this connection of the "fair value" of equitably distributed rights. Confronted with a homeless population silently swelling before our eyes, one is reminded of Anatole France's remark: the right "to sleep under a bridge" should not be the only one enjoyed by all.

If we read our constitutions in this material sense as texts concerning the realization of social justice, then the idea of *self-legislation* – according to which the addressees of the law should also understand themselves as its authors – takes on a *political dimension*, namely, that of a society which *acts upon itself*. Politicians of every stripe were guided by this dynamic understanding of the democratic process in constructing the welfare state in postwar Europe. The success of this project confirmed, in turn, the concept of self-transformation, that is, the idea of a society acting upon itself by political means. Today we are coming to the realization that this idea has thus far been realized only within the context of the nation-state. But if nation-states are running up against the limits of their own capacities in the changed context of a global economy and global society, then both the project of placing political controls on a globally unfettered capitalism and the sole example of a halfway-functioning mass democracy are being placed in question. Can this form of democratic self-transformation of modern societies be extended beyond national borders?

I propose to explore this question in three stages. We first need to clarify the interconnections between the nation-state and democracy and how this unique symbiosis is at present coming under increasing pressure. In light of this diagnosis, I will then briefly outline four political responses to the challenges posed by the postnational constellation; these responses also fix the coordinates of the current discussions of a "Third Way." Finally, this debate sets the stage for an offensive position on the future of the European Union. If the generally privileged citizens of our region wish to take the viewpoints of other countries and continents into account, then they will have to work toward deepening the federative aspect of the European

Union, with the cosmopolitan goal of creating the necessary preconditions for a global domestic politics.

Challenges for the Nation-State and Democracy

1 The trends which are currently commanding so much attention under the heading of "globalization" are transforming a historical constellation within which the state, society, and economy were more or less coextensive within the same national boundaries. The *international* economic system, in which states draw the boundaries between their domestic economies and foreign trade relations, is being transformed in the course of the globalization of markets into a *transnational* economy. The controversy surrounding the increased volume and intensity of cross-border trade, especially in industrial goods and services, like the discussion of the significance of the sharp increase in direct investment, concerns rates of flow within a single medium, not the shifts in the relation between the medium of the market and that of political power which are the really important factor. Especially relevant are the acceleration in the movement of global capital and the imperative assessment of national economic conditions by globally interconnected financial markets. These factors explain why today state actors no longer form the nodal points which lent global economic exchanges the character of interstate or international relations.[2] Today it is more true to say that states are embedded within markets than that national economies are embedded within the boundaries of states.

Needless to say, the ongoing erosion of borders is characteristic not just of the economy. A recently published study by David Held and colleagues on "global transformations" includes, in addition to chapters on global trade, financial markets, and multinational corporations with global production networks, chapters on global domestic politics, peacekeeping and organized violence, the rising tide of migration, the new media and communication networks, hybrid forms of culture, and identity conflicts resulting from the diffusion, superimposition, and interpenetration of cultural forms of life.[3] This ongoing broadly based "disembedding" of economy, society, and culture is impinging on the fundamental conditions of existence of a state system which was constructed on the territorial principle and which still accounts for the most important collective actors on the political stage. Restrictions on the room for maneuver of national governments simultaneously endanger the welfare state, and thereby also the sole example of the successful offsetting of the socially undesirable effects of capitalism. The democratic self-transformation of society with this goal has until now found institutional expression only within the framework of the nation-state. How can this affinity between the nation-state and democracy be explained?

2 Four preconditions must be met if an association of citizens is to be able to regulate their coexistence democratically and to shape social conditions by political means:

- there must be an effective political apparatus through which collectively binding decisions can be implemented;
- there must be a clearly defined "self" for the purposes of political self-determination and self-transformation to which collectively binding decisions can be ascribed;
- there must be a citizenry that can be mobilized for participation in political opinion-formation and will-formation oriented to the common good; and
- there must be an economic and social milieu in which a democratically programmed administration can provide legitimacy-enhancing steering and organization.

The instrumental requirement for effective political action was fulfilled by the administrative state, which established itself from the seventeenth century onwards, initially as a tax-levying state and later as a constitutional state, on the basis of a functional separation between public administrative power and civil society. The identity requirement for determining a collective subject capable of self-determination and self-transformation was fulfilled by the *sovereign territorial state* of classical international law, which defines the citizen body and governmental order in terms of the frontiers of a sovereign territory defended by military force. The requirement of active participation was fulfilled by the nation-state, which since the beginning of the nineteenth century produced an abstract form of solidarity among strangers through a combination of the cultural symbolism of "the people" and the republican status of citizens. Finally, the requirement that conditions of social life must be open to political transformation was fulfilled in the second half of the twentieth century by the *welfare state,* which secured the approximate fair value of equal civil rights under conditions of rapid economic growth.

This modern model of a territorial, national, and welfare state equipped with effective administrative power is especially adapted to democracy because a polity has to be adequately integrated in a political and cultural sense, and must be sufficiently autonomous in territorial, social, economic, and military respects – in other words, it must be independent of external influences – if the united citizenry is to be able to govern itself within the familiar forms of the constitutional state and to shape its society politically. Within nation-state democracies, both of these conditions were fulfilled to a greater or lesser degree through the congruence of state, society, and economy. But the postnational constellation is in effect putting an end to this constructive intermeshing of politics and the legal system with economic cycles and national traditions within the boundaries of territorial states. The trends summed up under the heading of "globalization" are not only jeopardizing the comparatively homogenous make-up of the population internally, and hence the prepolitical basis for the integration of citizens, through immigration and cultural segmentation. More decisive is the fact that states which are becoming increasingly *entangled* in the interdependencies of a global economy and global society are forfeiting their capacity for autonomous action, and with it their democratic substance.[4]

3 Leaving aside the issue of the empirical restrictions to the enduring formal sovereignty of states,[5] I shall here limit myself to three aspects of the erosion of the nation-state's prerogatives: (a) the decline in the state's capacities for control; (b) the growing deficits in legitimation in decision-making processes; and (c) the increasing inability to perform the kinds of steering and organizational functions which enhance legitimacy.

The *loss of autonomy* means, among other things, that individual states no longer possess sufficient power to protect their citizens from the external effects of decisions taken by other actors, or from the knock-on effects of processes which originate beyond their borders. The latter involve, on the one hand, "spontaneous border crossings" such as pollution, organized crime, security risks associated with large-scale technology, arms trafficking, epidemics, and so forth, and,

on the other, the reluctantly tolerated consequences of other states'
calculated policies, in whose formulation and legitimation many of
those who are affected by them are not involved – think, for example,
of the risks caused by nuclear reactors that are built outside a state's
borders and fail to meet its own safety standards.

Deficits in democratic legitimation arise whenever the set of those
involved in making democratic decisions fails to coincide with the
set of those affected by them. Democratic legitimacy is also harmed
in less obvious, but more durable, ways, when the growing need for
coordination due to increasing interdependence is successfully met
by intergovernmental agreements. In some areas of policy, the institutional embedding of the nation-state in a network of transnational
treaties and regimes does indeed create equivalents for competences
which have been forfeited at the national level.[6] But the more numerous and important the matters settled through interstate negotiations, the greater the number of political decisions that are withdrawn from democratic opinion-formation and will-formation, which
remain anchored exclusively in national arenas. In the European
Union, the largely bureaucratic decision-making process of the
experts in Brussels represents an example of the kind of democratic deficit that results from the shift away from national decision-
making bodies to interstate committees comprised of government
representatives.[7]

Debate focuses, however, on *the restriction of the capacities for intervention* heretofore mobilized by nation-states to implement legitimating social policies. With the widening gap between nation-states'
territorially limited room for action, on the one hand, and globalized
markets and accelerated capital flows, on the other, what Wolfgang
Streeck calls the "functional self-sufficiency of the domestic economy" is vanishing:

> Functional self-sufficiency should not be equated with autarky . . . [It]
> does not imply that a nation must possess a "full range" of products,
> but only a dependable supply of those complementary factors – above
> all, capital and organization – which the labor-supply generated by a
> society needs in order to produce.[8]

Footloose capital which has, so to speak, been released from its duty
to stay at home in its search for investment opportunities and
speculative profits can threaten to exercise its exit options whenever
a government imposes burdensome constraints on domestic business

conditions in an attempt to protect social standards, maintain job security, or preserve its ability to manage demand.

Under conditions of intense global competition to attract investment, high wages and benefits act as an incentive for economic rationalization. Mass layoffs underscore the increasing leverage of highly mobile corporations in contrast to the weakened position of locally operating labor unions. At the same time, national governments are losing their capacity to tap the tax resources of their economies, stimulate growth, and thereby secure vital bases for their legitimation. Demand-management politics have counterproductive external impacts on national economic cycles (as, for example, in the early 1980s under the first Mitterrand government) because international equities markets have now taken over the function of assessing national economic policies. In many European countries, the fact that markets are supplanting politics is expressed in the vicious circle of rising unemployment, strained social security systems, and shrinking social contributions. States are faced with the dilemma that the more urgent the need to replenish exhausted public finances through higher taxes on moveable property and economic stimulus packages, the harder it is becoming to implement such policies within the confines of the nation-state.

The Parameters of a Discussion

This challenge has called forth two blanket responses and two more nuanced ones. The polarization between the two camps which advance blanket arguments either (a) for or (b) against globalization and deterritorialization has led to a search for a "Third Way" in (c) comparatively defensive or (d) comparatively offensive variants.

(a) Support for globalization is based on the neoliberal orthodoxy which has ushered in the shift toward supply-side economic policies over the past decades. There has never been a more influential "epistemic community" than the Chicago School. It advocates the subordination of the state to the imperatives of a market-led integration of global society, and pleads for an "entrepreneurial state" that would abandon the project of decommodifying labor power and, more generally, the role of protector of lifeworld resources. A state enmeshed in the transnational economic system would abandon its citizens to the legally secured negative freedoms of global competition, while essentially confining itself to providing, in business-like fashion, infrastructures that promote entrepreneurial activity and make national economic conditions attractive from the point of view of profitability. This is not the place to address the assumptions informing neoliberal models or the venerable doctrinal dispute over the relationship between social justice and market efficiency.[9] Two objections, however, are thrown up by the premises of neoliberal theory itself.

Let us assume for the sake of argument that a fully liberalized global economy with unfettered mobility of all the factors of production (including labor power) were eventually to begin to operate in accordance with the conditions projected by advocates of globalization, namely, a world of harmoniously equilibrated production sites and the end state of a symmetrical division of labor. Even on this assumption, we would still have to accept a transitional period, both at the national and the global levels, marked not only by a drastic increase in social inequity and fragmentation, but also by the decay of moral standards and cultural infrastructures. Thus, from a temporal point of view, we must ask how long it would take to traverse the "valley of tears" and what sacrifices would have to be made along the way. How many people would have to suffer the fate of marginalization and being left by the wayside? How many irreplaceable achievements of civilization would be sacrificed to "creative destruction" in the process?

An equally unsettling question concerns the future of democracy. For the efficacy of the democratic procedures and institutional arrangements which promote the self-determination of the united citizenry, and which enable them to exercise political control over the conditions under which they live, can only diminish to the extent that the nation-state is shorn of functions and room for action without equivalents emerging at the supranational level. Wolfgang Streeck calls this the "declining purchasing power of the ballot" and sees "the danger that democratic leadership will decay into the ability to be elected on the basis of illusionary expectations concerning political power, while simultaneously taking care to ensure that one cannot be held responsible for failing to fulfill those exceptions."[10]

(b) On the other hand, the reaction to the devaluation of the nation-state and democracy has produced a coalition based on resistance to the social decline of the actual or potential losers of structural change and the disempowerment of the democratic state and its citizens. But the urgent desire to close the dike leads the "party of territoriality" (as Charles Maier puts it) to contest the egalitarian and universalistic foundations of democracy itself. At any rate, protectionist sentiment is grist to the mill of the ethnocentric rejection of diversity, the xenophobic rejection of others, and the anti-modern rejection of social complexity. Such sentiment is directed against whatever crosses national borders – the arms and drug-traffickers and Mafiosi who jeopardize national security, the flood of information and American movies which jeopardize national cultures, and the foreign investment, immigrant workers, and refugees who jeopardize national living standards.

Even giving due consideration to the rational kernel of these defensive reactions, it is easy to see why the nation-state cannot recover its old strength through isolationist policies. The liberalization of the global economy, which began after World War II and temporarily took the form of an "embedded liberalism" founded on a system of fixed exchange rates, has accelerated sharply since the demise of the Bretton Woods system. But this outcome was not inevitable. The systemic constraints currently exercised by the imperatives of a free trade regime that was undergirded by the creation of the World Trade Organization are the product of political voluntarism. Although the United States forced the pace of the various GATT rounds, GATT did not involve unilaterally imposed decisions, but negotiated path-dependent cumulative decisions that coordinated the undertakings of many individual governments to refrain from certain kinds of policies. And because global markets arose out of this kind of negative integration of many independent actors, projects to restore the *status quo ante* by *unilaterally* revoking the systematic result of concerted decisions would inevitably provoke sanctions.

The stand-off in the debate between the parties of globalization and territoriality has led to attempts to find a "Third Way." They branch off in two directions, toward (c) a defensive variant which assumes that the forces of global capitalism, having been unleashed, can no longer be tamed but can nevertheless be *cushioned* at the national level; and (d) an offensive variant that pins its hopes on the transformative power of a supranational politics that will gradually *catch up* with runaway markets.

(c) According to the defensive variant, the subordination of politics to the imperatives of a global society unified by the market is now irreversible. But the nation-state should not merely play a reactive role in creating favorable conditions for valorizing investment capital, but should also play an active role in promoting all attempts to provide citizens with the skills they need to compete. This new social policy is no less universalistic in its orientation than the old. However, its primary task is not to protect people from the typical risks of working life, but to equip them with the entrepreneurial qualities of "achievers" who are able to look out for themselves. The familiar adage about "helping people to help themselves" here acquires the economistic sense of a fitness program designed to whip everyone into shape to assume personal responsibility and to take the initiative in acquiring the skills necessary to compete successfully in the market – and not end up as "failures" who have to turn to the state for help: "social democrats have to shift the relationship between risk and security involved in the welfare state, to develop a society of 'responsible risk takers' in the spheres of government, business enterprise and labor markets. . . . Equality must contribute to diversity, not stand in its way."[11]

What bothers "old" socialists about the prospect held out by the "New Center" or "New Labor" is not only its normative chutzpah, but also the dubious empirical assumption that jobs, even when they do not take the form of traditional work relationships, remain "the key variable in social integration."[12] Both the secular trend toward productivity-enhancing and labor-saving technologies and the simultaneous rise in demand on the labor market, especially from women, render the opposite assumption that we are witnessing the "end of the full employment society" (Vobruba) not entirely farfetched. But if we abandon the political goal of full employment, then we must either scrap public standards of distributive justice or else consider alternatives that will put considerable strain on national business climates. Given the conditions prevailing in today's global economy, it is scarcely possible to implement cost-neutral projects such as redistributing the shrinking volume of available wage labor, promoting capital ownership among broad sectors of the population, or uncoupling a basic minimum wage pegged above current welfare levels from real earnings.

In normative terms, advocates of this "Third Way" have fallen into line with a form of liberalism that regards social equality solely from the standpoint of input, reducing it merely to equal opportunity.

Aside from this moral borrowing, public perception of the difference between Margaret Thatcher and Tony Blair has become blurred primarily because the "Newest Left" has assimilated the ethical conceptions of neoliberalism.[13] I have in mind its willingness to accommodate the ethos of a "lifestyle attuned to the global market,"[14] which expects all citizens to acquire the skills they need to become "entrepreneurs managing their own human capital."[15]

(d) Those who remain unwilling to take this step will consider a second, offensive variant of the Third Way. This perspective is guided by the idea that politics should take precedence over the logic of the market: "In a modern society, the extent to which the systematic logic of the market should be 'unleashed,' and where and in what framework the market should 'rule,' are ultimately matters that should be left to deliberative politics to decide."[16] This sounds like voluntarism, and indeed it is initially nothing more than a normative proposal that, in light of what has been said so far, can no longer be put into practice in a national context. However, the attempt to resolve the dilemma between disarming welfare state democracy and rearming the nation-state leads us to look to larger political units and transnational regimes capable of compensating for the nation-state's loss of functions without breaking the chain of democratic legitimacy. The European Union naturally first springs to mind as an example of a democracy functioning beyond the limits of the nation-state. To be sure, the creation of larger political entities does not in any way alter the process of competition for investment and jobs among states – that is, it does not challenge the primacy of market-led integration per se. Politics will succeed in "catching up" with globalized markets only if it eventually becomes possible to create an infrastructure capable of sustaining a global domestic politics without uncoupling it from democratic processes of legitimation.[17]

The notion that politics can "catch up" with markets by evolving in response to them is not, of course, meant to evoke the image of a power struggle between political and economic actors. The problematic consequences of a form of politics that equates society as a whole with market structures can be explained by the fact that money cannot be substituted for political power without qualification. The criteria for the exercise of legitimate power are different from those by which economic success is measured; for example, markets, unlike polities, cannot be democratized. A more appropriate image here would be that of competition between different media. The politics which creates markets is self-referential in that each step toward market deregulation entails a simultaneous disempowerment or self-restriction of political power as the medium for realizing collectively binding decisions. A "catch-up" politics inverts this process: it is a reflexive politics oriented to enhancing political power. And since the democratic production of political power depends on communicative processes which first authorize the use of power, political communication must also aim at a self-reflexive extension of a politics of this sort – at the cost of displacing a different regulatory mechanism.

Europe and the World

If we regard the development of the European Union to date from this perspective, we arrive at a paradoxical conclusion. The creation of new political institutions – the Brussels authorities, the European Court of Justice, and the European Central Bank – by no means implies a strengthening of politics per se. Monetary union represents the final step in a process which, notwithstanding Schumann's, de Gasperi's, and Adenauer's original program, can in retrospect be soberly described as "intergovernmental market-creation."[18] Today, the European Union constitutes a broad continental region which is spanned by a dense network of markets in the horizontal dimension, but is subject to relatively weak political regulation by indirectly legitimated authorities in the vertical dimension. Since member states, by transferring their sovereignty in currency matters to the European Central Bank, have lost their ability to steer their economies by adjusting exchange rates, the heightened competition we are likely to see within the single currency zone will give rise to problems of a new order of magnitude.

The hitherto nationally structured economies exhibit different levels of development and are marked by different economic styles. Until an integrated economy emerges from this heterogeneous mix, the interactions between Europe's individual economic zones, which are still embedded in different political systems, will lead to frictions. This holds in the first instance for weaker economies, which have to counteract their competitive disadvantages through wage-cutting, whereas stronger economies fear wage-dumping. An inauspicious scenario is being sketched for the social security systems remaining under national jurisdiction, which have very different structures and are already riven with conflicts. Whereas some countries fear the loss of their cost advantages, others fear downward adjustment. Europe is being confronted with the alternative of relieving these pressures through the market – ultimately, through competition between welfare regimes and national economies – or processing them by political means, that is, by attempting to bring about "harmonization" and gradual adjustment in major areas of welfare, employment, and tax policy. In essence, the issue is whether the institutional *status quo*, in which states balance out conflicting national interests through interstate negotiations, should be defended even at the cost of a race to the bottom, or whether the European Union should evolve beyond its present form of an alliance of states toward a genuine federation. Only in the latter case would it acquire the political strength to take market-correcting decisions and impose redistributive regulations.

Within the parameters of the current debate about globalization, neither the neoliberals nor the nationalists have much difficulty in choosing between these two alternatives. Whereas the despairing *Euroskeptics* are even more insistent on protection and exclusion now that monetary union has come into effect, *Market Europeans* are satisfied with monetary union as the completion of the European single market. In contrast with both of these positions, *Eurofederalists* aspire to a transformation of existing international accords into a political constitution in order to lend the decisions of the European Commission, the Council of Ministers, and the European Court of Justice their own basis of legitimacy. Those who adopt a *cosmopolitan* stance differ from all three positions. They regard a federal European state as a starting point for developing a transnational network of regimes that can pursue something akin to a global domestic politics, even without a world government. However, the central opposition between Eurofederalists and Market Europeans is complicated by the fact that the latter have entered into a tacit coalition with the erstwhile Euroskeptics who are now seeking a Third Way based on the *fait accompli* of monetary union. Blair and Schröder are, it would appear, no longer so far removed from Tietmeyer.[19]

The Market Europeans would like to preserve the European *status quo* because it sets the seal on the subordination of the fragmented nation-states to market-driven integration. Thus, a spokesman for the

Deutsche Bank can regard the debate over the alternative between an alliance of states, a "United States of Europe," and a European federal state as "academic": "In the context of the integration of economic zones, any distinction between civic and economic activity ultimately disappears. Indeed, this is the central goal being pursued by processes of integration."[20] From this vantage point, competition in Europe is supposed to "dispel the taboo" protecting national assets like the public credit sector or state social security systems, and gradually bring about their dissolution. However, the position of the Market Europeans rests on an assumption shared by the social democratic adherents of the nation-state who now want to pursue a Third Way: "Overcoming the restrictions on state power in the age of globalization is impossible; [globalization] . . . demands above all that we strengthen the forces of freedom in civil society," namely, "the individual initiative and sense of personal responsibility of citizens."[21] This shared premise explains the switch in alliances. Former Euroskeptics today support Market Europeans in their defense of the European *status quo*, even though from different motives and with different goals. They do not want to dismantle the state's welfare policies, but want to redirect them toward investments in human capital – and, let us add, they do not want the social "shock absorbers" to fall entirely into private hands.

Thus the debate between neoliberals and Eurofederalists becomes entangled with one between defensive and offensive variants of the Third Way which is smoldering in the social democratic camp – between, let us say, Schröder and Lafontaine. This debate concerns not only the question of whether the European Union can recover the leeway that nation-states have lost by harmonizing divergent national fiscal, social, and economic policies. After all, the European economic zone is still relatively insulated from global competition, thanks to a tightly woven regional network of trade relations and direct investments. The debate between Euroskeptics and Eurofederalists hinges above all on whether the EU – in view of the diversity of its member states and their peoples, cultures, and languages – can ever acquire the character of an authentic state, or whether it is destined to remain the prisoner of neo-corporatist negotiation systems.[22] Eurofederalists seek to enhance the governability of the Union, so as to make possible the pan-European implementation of policies and regulations that will oblige member states to coordinate their actions, even when this leads to redistributive effects. From this viewpoint, any extension of the Union's capacity for political action must go hand-in-hand with a broadening of its basis of legitimation.

It is beyond dispute that the *sine qua non* for a democratic will-formation on a pan-European scale that is capable of sustaining and legitimating positively coordinated and effective redistributive policies is greater solidarity at the base. Civic solidarity, which has hitherto been limited to the nation-state, will have to be widened to encompass all citizens of the Union, so that, for example, Swedes and Portuguese will be ready to vouch for one another. Only then can they be reasonably expected to support a roughly equal minimum wage, or, more generally, the creation of equal conditions for forging individual life plans, which will, to be sure, continue to exhibit national features. Skeptics doubt whether this is possible, arguing that there is no such thing as a European "people" capable of constituting a European state.[23] However, peoples first come into being with their state constitutions. Democracy itself is a juridically mediated form of political integration. Of course, democracy depends in turn on a political culture shared by all citizens. But if one bears in mind that, in the European states in the nineteenth century, national consciousness and civic solidarity – the first modern form of collective identity – were produced only gradually with the help of national historiography, mass communication, and universal conscription, then there is no call for defeatism. If this artificial form of "solidarity among strangers" owes its existence to a historically momentous advance in abstraction from local and dynastic consciousness to national and democratic consciousness, why then should it not be possible for this learning process to continue beyond national borders?

Major hurdles undoubtedly remain. A constitution will not be enough. It can only initiate the democratic processes in which it must then take root. Since agreements between member states will remain a factor even in a politically constituted union, a European federal state will, in any case, have to take a different form from national federal states and cannot simply copy their legitimation processes.[24] A European party system will take shape only to the extent that the existing parties first debate the future of Europe in their own national arenas and in the process discover interests that transcend national borders. This discussion must be conducted in inter-linked national public spheres throughout Europe in a synchronized fashion; that is, the same issues must be discussed simultaneously, so

as to foster the emergence of a European civil society with its interest groups, non-governmental organizations, civic initiatives, and so
forth. Transnational mass media can, in turn, establish a multi-lingual
communicative context only if the national school systems ensure
that Europeans have a common grounding in foreign languages. If
that happens, the legacies of a common European history, radiating
outwards from their scattered national centers, will gradually reunite
in a common political culture.

Let me conclude with a few words on the cosmopolitan perspective opened up by this development. A federal European state would,
on account of its broadened economic base, at best achieve
economies of scale, and therewith advantages in global competition.
But if the federative project aimed only to field another global player
with the clout of the United States, it would remain particularistic
and merely endow what in asylum policy has come to be known as
"Fortress Europe" with a new, economic dimension. Neoliberals could
even counter by beating the drum of the "morality of the market,"
vaunting the "impartial judgment" of a world market that has, after
all, already given the emerging economies a chance to exploit their
relative cost advantages, relying on their own forces to close a gap
which well-meaning development programs have proven incapable
of overcoming. I need not elaborate on the social costs implied by
the dynamics of this model of development.[25] But it is hard to gainsay
the argument that supranational groupings which become political
entities capable of acting on a global scale are normatively unobjectionable only if this first step – the one leading to their creation – is
followed by a second.

This prompts the question of whether the small group of globally
influential political actors can, within the framework of a reformed
world organization, so extend the present loose network of transnational regimes that they can then use it to effect a change toward a
global domestic politics without a world government.[26] A political
project of this kind would have to be conducted with a view to bringing about harmonization instead of lock-step conformity, without
permanently conferring a false legitimacy on the temporary multiplicity of ecological and social standards. The long-term goal would
have to be the gradual elimination of the social divisions and stratification of world society without jeopardizing cultural distinctiveness.

7

Does Europe Need
a Constitution?

The expectations and demands of the "Europeans of the First Hour" who pushed for European unification immediately after World War II[1] stand in peculiar contrast to those who confront the task of continuing that project today. What is striking is not just the marked difference in rhetorical mood, but also the contrasting goals. Whereas the pioneering generation spoke of a "United States of Europe" without flinching from a comparison with the United States, the current discussion eschews such models. Even the word "federalism" has become suspect.[2] Larry Siedentop's recent book, which created a stir in England, exhibits a mindset much closer to Chirac's caution than the vision of Joschka Fischer. As he puts it:

> A great constitutional debate need not involve a prior commitment to federalism as the most desirable outcome in Europe. It may reveal that Europe is in the process of inventing a new political form, something more than a confederation but less than a federation – an association of sovereign states which pool their sovereignty only in very restricted areas or to varying degrees, an association which does not seek to have the coercive power to act directly on individuals in the fashion of nation-states.[3]

Does this shift in political climate simply reflect a healthy realism, the product of a decades-long learning process, or is it not rather a sign of a debilitating timidity, if not outright defeatism?

Siedentop misses the mark when he complains of the lack of an inspired constitutional debate that fires the imaginations of the peoples of Europe. For our situation is not comparable to that of either the American federalists[4] or the delegates to the Assemblée nationale. At the end of the eighteenth century, the Founding Fathers in Philadelphia and the revolutionary citizens in Paris were initiators of, and participants in, an extraordinary undertaking without historical precedent. After 200 years of constitutional practice, we are not merely treading well-worn paths; the constitutional question is no longer the key to the problems we have to solve. Indeed, the challenge is less to invent something new than to conserve the great achievements of the European nation-state beyond its frontiers in a new form. What is new is only the entity which will arise through these endeavors. What must be conserved are the standards of living, the opportunities for education and leisure, and the social space for personal self-realization which are necessary to ensure the fair value of individual liberty, and thereby make democratic participation possible. This "materialization" of constitutional guarantees already noted by Max Weber means that current debates over the "future of Europe" are now increasingly the preserve of highly specialized and complex discourses among economists and social scientists, and especially political scientists, rather than the domain of constitutional lawyers and political philosophers. By the same token, we should not underestimate the symbolic importance of the sheer fact that a constitutional debate is now under way. The Euro alone is not sufficient to inspire enthusiasm for Europe as a political community in the minds of Europeans. The intergovernmental agreement in Maastricht lacks the symbolic power which can only be generated by a political founding act.

At the end of this essay I will offer some brief reflections on the European constitution. To begin with, I will examine the supporting arguments that continue to speak for an energetic continuation of the project of European unification. I will then address the two central questions of the "Euroskeptics": first, whether European societies currently actually fulfill the preconditions for a federalist expansion of the European Union and, second, assuming that they do, who could carry out such a political project, and with what constitutional aims, given current levels of popular resistance to it.

Why Should Europe Pursue an "Ever-Closer Union"?

I will discuss the justification for an offensive posture on the future of the European Union under two aspects: first, that of political goals and, second, that of the problems with which we are inescapably confronted as a result of political decisions already taken.

1 The goals of the EU's founding generation (Schumann, de Gasperi, and Adenauer) have lost much of their original relevance. However, the EU elites have in the meantime replaced the original goals with a different agenda.

The strongest driving force for European unity until the Kohl generation was the desire to put an end to the bloody history of warfare in Europe. A further motive – one shared by Adenauer, as it happens – was to promote Germany's integration into Europe, in an effort to placate the historically well-founded mistrust of a nation at the heart of Europe which remained politically unstable but was soon to reinvigorate its economy. Although all sides now agree that the pacification of Europe has been definitively achieved, the goal of securing peace remains relevant in a very different context. For, in the course of the war in Kosovo, a subtle but important difference emerged between the justifications offered for humanitarian intervention. The United States and Britain viewed the deployment of NATO forces in terms of their broader national preferences for promoting a politics of human rights. The continental European states, by contrast, appeared to take their orientation from the anticipated principles of a future cosmopolitan legal order, rather than from present exigencies of political order as understood by a globally oriented superpower.[5] In view of the structural transformations of international relations, and the emergence of transnational networks and complete new kinds of challenges, there are good reasons for the European Union, backed by its own military forces, to speak with a single voice on issues of foreign and security policy, and thereby bring a stronger influence of its own to bear in NATO and the UN Security Council.

The second goal, the integration of a Germany still eyed with suspicion into a peaceful Europe, may have lost its salience with the growing stability of democratic institutions and the spread of liberal attitudes in the Federal Republic, even though the reunification of 82 million Germans has revived old fears of a relapse into the imperial fantasies and traditions of the German Reich. I need not pursue this topic any further here, since neither of the original motives for integration would today still count as a sufficient justification for a deeper integration of Europe. In any event, the "Carolingian" heritage invoked by the conservative founder generation, with its explicit appeal to the Christian West, has vanished.

Of course, there was always a third strand in European integration, namely, the straightforward economic interest in the creation of a single market. Since the Coal and Steel Community of 1951 and the foundation of the European Economic Community and Euratom in 1958, more and more countries have become integrated through the free exchange of people, goods, capital, and services, a process now completed with the creation of the single market and the introduction of the single currency. The European Union currently provides the framework for an ever denser network of trade relations, direct investment, and transactions of all kinds. Europe has achieved a strong and increasingly influential position alongside the United States and Japan. On the other hand, rational calculations of profits and of differential competitive advantages can provide only a limited form of legitimation. Economic achievements can, at best, stabilize the *status quo*, even making allowance for the symbolic impact of the unifying effect of the Euro in the everyday lives of consumers.

Economic motives alone cannot mobilize popular political support for the risky project of a European union worthy of the name. This further goal requires the legitimation of shared values.[6] Of course, the legitimacy of a political regime also depends on its efficiency. But political innovations, such as the construction of a state of nation-states, require political mobilization for goals which fire people's imaginations rather than just appeal to their interests. Constitution-making has hitherto involved historical responses to crisis situations. But where are the crises facing today's generally prosperous and peaceful Western European societies? In Central and Eastern Europe, by contrast, the transitional societies which aspire to membership in the EU are confronted with the daunting challenges resulting from the collapse of socialism; but their answer has been the return to the nation-state. In these countries, in particular, there is no enthusiasm for a transfer of parts of their recently regained national sovereignty to European institutions.

The current lack of motivation for political integration on both sides makes the insufficiency of purely economic justifications for European unification all the more manifest. If national majorities within the member states are to be won over for a transformation of the political *status quo*, economic motives must be connected with ideas of a completely different kind – let us say, with the idea of preserving a threatened culture and way of life. The overwhelming majority of European citizens feel united in the interest in preserving the way of life which they were fortunate enough to develop in the regions on this side of the Iron Curtain during the third quarter of the last century, that is, during what Hobsbawm has called the "golden age." Of course, rapid economic growth provided the basis for a welfare state that provided the framework for the regeneration of postwar European societies. But the most important outcome of this regeneration was the production of ways of life which fostered the renewal of the wealth and national diversity of a centuries-old culture in attractive forms under conditions of security and prosperity.

The economic advantages of European unification can count as valid arguments for the further expansion of the EU only against the background of the attractive force of a culture extending far beyond the economic sphere. Threats to this way of life, and the desire to protect it, are spurs to a vision of Europe that is once again capable of responding inventively to the challenges it now faces. In his wonderful speech of May 28, 2001, the French Prime Minister spoke of this "European way of life" as the content of a political project:

> Until recently, the efforts of the Union were concentrated on the creation of monetary and economic union. . . . But today we need a broader perspective if Europe is not to decay into a mere market and dissolve in globalization. For Europe is much more than a market. It stands for a model for society that developed historically.[7]

Economic globalization, whether we interpret it as the acceleration of long-running trends or as the transition to a new transnational form of capitalism, shares with all processes of accelerated modernization some disquieting features. Periods of rapid structural change give rise to sharper inequalities in the distribution of social costs. Inequalities in status between the winners and losers in processes of modernization increase, accompanied by the general expectation of higher short-term costs in return for greater long-term gains. Yet the last wave of economic globalization did not stem from any inherent evolution of the system. Since the globalization of markets is the result of deliberate political decisions, such as the GATT rounds and the creation of the World Trade Organization, it must also be possible to counteract the undesired social consequences of these decisions, not indeed by reversing the process, but by complementary corrective social and economic policies.

As a general rule, such policies must be tailored to the needs of different social groups.[8] For short-term losers, gaps in employment can be bridged by investments in education and retraining programs, as well as temporary transfers, whereas the long-run losers can receive compensation in the form of, for example, a negative income tax or some other form of basic wage uncoupled from employment status. Of course, redistributive programs are difficult to implement, especially as the losers in processes of modernization are no longer members of an industrial labor force with a strong veto position. For the political decision on whether or not to maintain an appropriate level of *general* social welfare as a barrier to the social segmentation of fringe groups, and to social exclusion in general, increasingly depends on considerations of justice, and especially on the sensitivity of broad sectors of society to the visible effects of injured civic solidarity. But such normative orientations move majorities only to the extent that they remain anchored in the traditions of the dominant political culture.

The latter assumption is not entirely unfounded in European countries in which the political traditions of the workers' movements, Christian social doctrine, and social liberalism still ensure that notions of social solidarity have a certain resonance. The literature on comparative cultural analysis attests to a distinctive European system of values combining private individualism and public collectivism. Thus Göran Therborn claims:

> [T]he European road to and through modernity has also left a certain legacy of social norms, reflecting European experiences of class and gender. . . . Collective bargaining, trade unions, public social services, the rights of women and children are all held more legitimate in Europe than in the rest of the contemporary world. They are expressed in social documents of the EU and of the Council of Europe.[9]

In their public self-representations, at any rate, the major political parties still draw on this background. They cling to a substantive conception of democratic citizenship and are judged by relatively inclusive social and political goals, even in an era of policies geared to ensuring national economic competitiveness.

Even granting this assumption, of course, there remains the question of why national governments should not be in a better position than a cumbersome Brussels bureaucracy to implement effective countervailing policies and corrective programs. At issue here is the controversial question of how economic globalization is affecting the scope for action of national governments. I myself have emphasized the shift toward a "postnational" constellation.[10] In the meantime, a number of objections have been raised against this thesis.[11] There is no direct relation, it is observed, between the globalization of markets and a decrease in the autonomy of states, nor is there necessarily an inverse relation between levels of employment and of social welfare:

- National governments, even independently of growing global pressures from outside, have had to learn to play a less dominant, more mediating role in their dealings with influential social actors within national arenas. The literature in social economics underlines the cooperative traits that states acquire once they are drawn into negotiating regimes where they must work with more or less self-assertive parties. Apparently, the state, although it retains exclusive control over the means of legitimate violence, must increasingly switch from an imperative style to one of convincing and persuading.[12]
- Although national governments may be compelled to lower corporate tax under the pressure of international economic competition, the most recent comparative studies seem to indicate that they still enjoy a range of options in policy areas that have an immediate impact on the covariant relationship between levels of employment and of social welfare.[13]

Of course, such arguments are far from invalidating two general assumptions:

- that national governments are becoming increasingly enmeshed in transnational networks, and are thereby becoming ever more dependent on political outcomes negotiated under asymmetrical relations of power; and
- that national governments, whatever policies they pursue, must adapt to the constraints imposed by deregulated markets and that they must accept growing inequalities in the distribution of the social product, in response to the forced decrease in corporate tax rates and shrinking public finances.

Hence, there remains the problem of whether our smaller or medium-sized nation-states, left to their own devices, can preserve their capacity to withstand a creeping assimilation to the social model being foisted upon them by the currently dominant economic regime. If I may be permitted a polemical exaggeration, this model is characterized by four features: first, by an anthropological image of human beings as rational choosers and entrepreneurs who exploit their own labor power; second, by the moral image of a post-egalitarian society that has resigned itself to marginalization and exclusion; third, by the economic image of a democracy that reduces citizenship to the status of membership of a market society and redefines the state as a service-provider for clients and customers; and, finally, by the strategic notion that the best form of politics is one that renders itself redundant.

These are the building blocks of a neoliberal worldview, which, if I am not mistaken, does not sit well with the traditional normative self-understanding of Europeans. Which interpretation of the project of European unification does this diagnosis support? To the extent that Europeans wish to counterbalance the undesirable social consequences of growing distributive inequities and seek a certain regulation of the global economy, they must take an interest in the power to shape institutions and outcomes which would accrue to a politically effective European Union within the circle of global players. Helmut Schmidt recently complained that Europe lacks a common finance minister who could represent it at summit meetings of the Group of Seven, for example. According to Schmidt, the twelve Euro states should pool their stakes in the IMF, the World Bank, and the Bank for International Settlements: "A common representation for all of the Euro states would be an effective platform from which the EU could advocate a stable regulation of the global financial markets and an effective oversight of banks which engage in irresponsible speculations."[14]

The vision of two Europe experts at the Free University in Brussels, Mario Telò and Paul Mignette, also points in this direction:

> The European Union is now being challenged to develop a better balance between deregulation and reregulation than national rules have been able to achieve. . . . The Union may be seen as a laboratory in which Europeans are striving to implement the values of justice and solidarity in the context of an increasing global economy.[15]

With a view to a future shaped by a highly stratified global society, we Europeans have a legitimate interest in making our voices heard in an international concert that has until now been playing from a completely different score.

Of course, this perspective arouses the suspicion that it represents a partisan – specifically, a social democratic – reading of the European project. One might object that any substantive interpretation will be biased and polarizes advocates and opponents. But given the weak motivation and growing skepticism concerning European unification, mobilization of the base is inconceivable without polarizing opinions. And this strategy is unobjectionable from a normative point of view because its success would be of a procedural nature. A Europe equipped with a political constitution and with stronger institutions would strengthen the capacity for collective action without prejudicing decisions concerning its ultimate direction. An expansion in political competences is a necessary, though not a sufficient, condition for making corrections to the global economic regime that some of us in the Eurofederalist camp regard as desirable.

2 But even discounting such far-reaching normative goals, there are other kinds of reasons for actively promoting the European project. One way or another we have to come to terms with problems resulting from the accumulation of the unintended consequences of past political decisions. The current debate over reform was triggered by the dilemmas of the "enlargement crisis."[16] The EU put itself under pressure to reform by fixing a date for the accession of the Eastern European states. For the enlargement of the Union by twelve new, socially and economically relatively heterogeneous countries increases the complexity of the issues in need of regulation and coordination which cannot be mastered without further integration or "deepening" of the Union. The Nice Treaty has not resolved this reform deadlock. To date, the problem of enlargement has failed to function as a lever for resolving the deeper structural problems. These problems arise from the disproportion between dense economic and comparatively loose political networks, on the one hand, and the democratic deficits of decision-making processes in Brussels, on the other.

The EU member states have largely retained their competences not only in the domains of cultural and education policy, but in those of finance, economic, and social policy as well. But in transferring their monetary sovereignty to the presumptively unpolitical European Central Bank, they have divested themselves of an important instrument of state intervention. Now that the monetary union has completed the process of economic integration, the need for a "harmonization" of the policies of the individual states in a range of areas is growing. The various nation-states have different legal traditions, different regimes in the area of social policy, and different neo-corporatist arrangements and tax systems. Thus they tend to respond differently to the same stimuli and challenges, with the result that the interferences between the side-effects of their respective policies often have counterproductive consequences. (A trivial example is the uncoordinated way in which neighboring governments reacted to the mass protests against the sudden rise in oil and petrol prices in September 2000.) National governments are still competing with one another over the best way to adapt their welfare systems to demographic shifts and the imperatives of a changed global economic situation. At the same time, they have to reach an agreement on minimal social standards, and hence take the first step in the direction of a social union which, according to Jacques Delors, would promote a convergence in levels of contributions and payments in the medium term.

Yet the discrepancy between well-advanced economic and lagging political integration could be overcome by a policy that aims at constructing higher-level political agencies in an attempt to keep pace with the deregulated markets. From this perspective, the European project can be seen as the common effort of the national governments to recover in Brussels something of the capacity for intervention that each of them has lost at home. This, at any rate, is the view of Lionel Jospin, who has called for common economic regulation of the Euro-zone and, in the long term, for harmonization of corporate taxes within it.[17]

The coordination of broader areas of policy would, of course, mean a concentration of competences, which would merely exacerbate another dilemma. The democratic deficit of the Brussels authorities is already a source of growing political dissatisfaction among the broader population. This is true not only of smaller states like Denmark and Ireland, and those which have rejected membership of the EU for the present, such as Switzerland and Norway. Until now, the decisions of the Commission and the Council of Ministers have essentially been legitimated through the channels of the existing nation-states. This level of legitimation corresponds to a form of intergovernmental authority based on international treaties and was sufficient as long as policies designed to create markets were called for. But insofar as the Council of Ministers and the Commission can no longer limit themselves to the negative form of coordination effected by policies of non-interference, but must make the transition to the positive coordination involved in interventions with redistributive effects, the lack of a pan-European civic solidarity becomes manifest. By some estimates, the implementation of European directives already affects 70 percent of national legislative processes without these matters being exposed to public debate in the national arenas, to which in any case only the holders of European passports have access.

The sheer intensity of decisions at the European level, the opacity of the processes by which they come about, and the lack of opportunity for citizens to participate in them are generating mistrust at the base. Claus Offe has explored the issues and regulatory needs which arouse fears in the individual nations and provoke rivalries among them. People are primarily concerned about fiscal redistribution effects that could disadvantage their fellow-countrymen while benefiting other nations. An additional source of fears concerns flows of immigrants from, and flows of investment to, foreign countries. A further source of worry is the idea that unchecked competition with societies with different levels of productivity has harmful consequences for one's own society. Offe describes the current relations among the EU member states as a "peaceful state of nature" that could only be overcome by a European "state-building," though one which should not reproduce the template of the nation-state. But even such a skeptical observer as Offe comes to the conclusion that we need an "organizational power" which lays the foundation of a European society through "positive integration."[18]

Can the European Union Acquire the Characteristics of a State?

So much for the reasons which justify the political project of a federalist European Constitution that is something more than a mere confederation. An entirely different question is whether Europe can fulfill the necessary empirical preconditions for the new, still unclear design of a state of nation-states. I will first address a familiar objection of the Euroskeptics, before turning to the preconditions of a political union that would assume the qualities of a state.

1 Euroskeptics reject a shift in the basis of legitimation of the Union from international treaties to a European constitution with the argument "that there is as yet no European people."[19] What is apparently missing is the requisite subject of the constitutional founding process, that is, the "people" in the collective singular which is capable of constituting itself as a nation of citizens. This "no demos thesis" has been criticized on both conceptual and empirical grounds. The civic nation must not be confused with a community of fate shaped by common descent, language, and history. For this fails to capture the voluntaristic character of a civic nation whose collective identity exists neither prior to, nor independently of, the democratic process from which it springs.

The contrast between civic and ethnic conceptions of the "nation" also reflects the great accomplishment of the democratic nation-state which, in creating the status of citizenship, first produced an entirely new, abstract, and legally mediated form of social solidarity. From a historical point of view, this first modern form of social integration extending beyond personal acquaintance arose in the context of new modes of communication made possible by the media. Although shared languages and cultural forms of life did indeed facilitate the development of national consciousness, the fact that democracy and the nation-state developed in tandem does not support the conclusion that the people must have preceded the republic. Rather, this dual development reveals a circular process in which national consciousness and democratic citizenship reciprocally stabilized each other. Both together first brought forth the novel phenomenon of a civic solidarity that henceforth constitutes the cement of national societies. National consciousness arose as much from the mass communication of newspaper readers as from the mass mobilizations of draftees and voters. It was shaped by the construction of patriotic national histories no less than by the public discourse of political parties competing for influence and power.

The history of the emergence of the European nation-states teaches us that the new forms of national identity have an artificial character that took shape only under the specific conditions of a long historical process which spanned the entire nineteenth century. This process of identity-formation owes its existence to a painful process of abstraction through which local and dynastic loyalties were ultimately transformed into the self-consciousness of democratic citizens as belonging to one and the same nation. But if this is correct, then there is no reason to assume that the formation of this kind of civic solidarity must come to a halt at the boundaries of the nation-state.

2 The conditions under which national consciousness arose nevertheless serve as a reminder of the empirical preconditions that must be fulfilled if such an improbable process of identity-formation is to be able to transcend national borders. These comprise the need for a European civil society, the construction of a pan-European political public sphere, and the creation of a political culture that all EU citizens can share. These three functional requirements for a democratically constituted European Union can serve as points of reference for complex, yet convergent developments. By exerting a kind of catalytic effect, a constitution can accelerate these processes and direct them toward the point of convergence. Europe has to apply to itself once again the logic of the circular process in which the democratic state and the nation mutually constituted each other, only this time in a reflexive manner, so to speak. It would begin with a referendum on the constitution, which would touch off a large-scale debate throughout Europe. For the constitution-founding process itself represents a unique medium of transnational communication which has the potential to become a self-fulfilling prophecy. A European constitution would not only bring to light the shift in powers which has already quietly taken place, but would also foster new constellations of power.

· Let us first consider the civil society actors. Once the European Union had gained fiscal autonomy through the power to levy taxes, and once the Commission had shared the functions of government with a permanent European Council, the Parliament in Strasburg, by performing a competing legislative function, would also be better able to exercise its already impressive powers and thereby win greater attention for itself. The full budgetary powers of classical representative assemblies would not even be necessary for this to happen. The axis of politics would shift more markedly from the national capitals toward Brussels and Strasburg. This would also hold for the activities of political parties, interest groups, and business organizations, for the lobbying efforts of professional associations and cultural and scientific organizations, and also for the "pressure from the street," that is, the protests which would no longer be initiated only by farmers and truck drivers but also by civic initiatives and movements.

In addition, interests organized along economic, occupational, religious, ideological, class, regional, and gender lines would tend to merge across national boundaries. The perceived transnational overlapping of parallel interests and value-orientations would foster the emergence of a European party system and cross-border networks. In this way, territorial forms of organizations would be displaced by functional principles of organization, giving rise to associative relations which would form the core of a pan-European civil society.

Of course, the democratic deficit can only be redressed by the simultaneous emergence of a European political public sphere in which the democratic process is embedded. In complex societies, democratic legitimacy results from the interplay of institutionalized consultation and decision-making processes, on the one hand, and informal public processes of communication in which opinions are formed via the mass media, on the other. In constitutional democracies, the infrastructure of the public sphere ideally plays the role of transforming problems of concern to society as a whole into the focal topics of discourses so that citizens have an opportunity to relate simultaneously to the same issues in similar terms, and hence to take affirmative or negative stances on the associated controversies. The for the most part implicit and diffuse "yes" or "no" stances on more or less well-informed and well-grounded alternatives constitute the microscopic particles which, on the one hand, aggregate into influential opinions on current issues and, on the other, precipitate out into more enduring attitudes and democratic election results.

At present, such arenas for the formation of public opinions and collective decisions still exist only within nation-states. But the missing European public sphere should not be imagined as the domestic public sphere writ large. It can arise only insofar as the circuits of communication within the national arenas open themselves up to one another while themselves remaining intact. The stratification of various levels of political opinion-formation – regional, national, and federal – assigned to different strata within a multilevel political architecture suggests the false image of a super-public sphere superimposed on the national public spheres. On the contrary, the mutually translated processes of communication within the national spheres must intersect in such a way that the relevant contributions from each arena are absorbed osmotically by all the others. In this way, European issues which were heretofore negotiated and decided upon without the involvement of the public could find their way into the interconnected national arenas.

The pressing question "Can the European Union become a sphere of publics?"[20] can only be answered from a transnational perspective. If we search for English-language newspapers with a multinational readership, all we find are the *Financial Times* and *The Economist* read by the business elite, or the *International Herald Tribune* (including a digest of the *Frankfurter Allgemeine Zeitung*) read by a political class – not exactly European papers. These media outlets do not offer a promising model for cross-border communication. In the audio-visual sector, the bilingual television channel Arte represents a more convincing model, though it remains inspired by the image of a supra-national public sphere in which different nationalities participate. As an alternative, let us imagine that the established mode of publica-tion during summit meetings of the European Council were to become standard. In this way, the questions affecting the common interests of citizens across Europe could be made accessible to them. The national media of one country would merely have to take up and comment on the substance of controversies being conducted in other member countries. Opinions and counterpositions could then develop in parallel around the same kinds of issues, information, and arguments in all member countries, regardless of where they origi-nate. The fact that these horizontal, back-and-forth flows of com-munications would have to pass through the filter of mutual translations would in no way impair the essential function of cross-border, but shared, political opinion and will-formation.

Within the European Union there are at present 13 different offi-cially recognized languages.[21] At first sight, this linguistic pluralism seems to represent an insurmountable obstacle to the creation of a pan-European political community. The official multilingualism of EU policy is an indispensable expression of the reciprocal recogni-tion of the equal worth and integrity of the different national cul-tures. But this guarantee makes it all the easier to use English as a face-to-face working language whenever the parties involved do not share some other common language.[22] It is worth mentioning in this connection that smaller nations like the Netherlands, Denmark,

Sweden, and Norway provide good examples of school systems which have established English as a second first language among the population as a whole.[23]

A pan-European public sphere depends on the vital inputs of actors within civil society, but it must at the same time be embedded in a shared political culture. Even though intellectuals apparently did not feel any need to reflect on the idea and nature of Europe until the nineteenth century,[24] an anxious debate has been conducted about it ever since.[25] The anxiety arises from the fact that the achievements of European culture have become diffused across the globe. This is as true of evangelical Christianity as of the secular achievements of science and technology, Roman law and the Napoleonic Code, the nation state, democracy, and human rights. Let me mention just two specific experiences which have had a remarkable resonance in Europe. In the course of its history, Europe, more than any other culture, has confronted deep structural conflicts and tensions, in the social as well as the temporal dimension. This fact no doubt also explains Europe's aggressive expansionist tendencies and its high potential for violence. What interests me in the present context, however, is that Europeans have also responded in productive ways to these challenges, and in the process have learned two principal lessons: to live with long-term, stabilized conflicts and to adopt a reflexive attitude toward their own traditions.

In the social dimension, modern Europe has developed institutional arrangements for productively resolving intellectual, social, and political conflicts. In the course of painful and often fatal struggles, Europe has learned how to cope with the rivalry between ecclesiastical and secular powers, the cleavage between faith and knowledge, the endemic conflicts between religious confessions, the antagonisms between city and country, court and city, town and gown, and, ultimately, with the enmity and rivalry between belligerent nation-states. Our success lay not in solving these conflicts, but rather in stabilizing them and transforming them into a source of innovative energies through ritualization. This dialectical mode of problem-solving finds conceptual expression in the idea of recognizing "reasonable disagreements," that is, the rational expectation that in many cases agreement will not be forthcoming.

In the temporal dimension, Europe following the French Revolution responded to the cleavages, discontinuities, and tensions which are intrinsic to processes of modernization with the institution of ideological competition between political parties. The classic party system ensured the reproduction of a broad spectrum of conservative, liberal, and socialist interpretations of capitalist modernization. In the course of the heroic assimilation of an incomparably rich Jewish, Greek, Roman, and Christian heritage, Europe learned how to adopt a sensitive attitude toward the Janus face of modernity. The challenge is to take account of two conflicting aspects of modernity at once: on the one hand, the deplorable losses incurred by the disintegration of protective traditional forms of life and, on the other, the promise of future benefits resulting from present processes of creative destruction. This challenge acted as a spur to critical reflection on the blind spots in our own, supposedly universalistic, vision, and to a progressive decentering of perspectives which are repeatedly recognized as selective. This kind of reflexivity is not proof against disastrous forms of Eurocentrism – it is merely its other, better side.

At any rate, the egalitarian and individualistic universalism which continues to shape our normative self-understanding is not the least of the achievements of modern Europe. The fact that capital punishment is still practiced elsewhere serves as a reminder of specific features of our normative consciousness:

> The Council of Europe, with the European Convention on Human Rights, and its European Social Charter, have transformed Europe into an area of human rights, more specific and more binding than in any other area of the world. . . . The clear and general European support for an International Crimes Tribunal, again in contrast to US fears, is also in the same line.[26]

The common core of a European identity is constituted more by the character of the learning processes it has gone through than by their results. It is memory of the moral abyss into which the excesses of nationalism led us that lends our current commitment the status of an accomplishment. This historical background could serve to smooth the transition to a postnational democracy founded on mutual recognition of the differences between proud national cultures. Neither "assimilation" nor mere "coexistence" (in the sense of a fragile *modus vivendi*) fit well with this history which has taught us how to construct ever more abstract forms of "solidarity among strangers."

The new awareness of commonality has found expression in the EU Charter of Fundamental Rights. The parties to the Convention reached agreement on this document in a remarkably short space of time.[27] Even though the sixth meeting of the European Council in Nice only "proclaimed" this schedule of basic rights and stopped short of adopting it as law, the Charter will influence the rulings of the European Court of Justice. Until now, the Court has been primarily concerned with the implications of the "four freedoms" of the EU internal market. With its social requirements, by contrast, the Charter goes beyond this narrow economic perspective. The document shows in an exemplary way what binds European citizens in a normative sense. On developments in genetic technology, for example, Article 3 of the Charter lays down the right of each person to respect for his or her physical and mental integrity, and prohibits all forms of positive eugenics and the reproductive cloning of human beings.

What is Euro-Federalism?

Let us assume for the moment that there are compelling reasons for continuing to pursue the project of European unification and that the empirical preconditions for a politically constituted Europe can in principle be fulfilled. Even so, there still remains a gap between project and realization which can only be bridged by the political will of competent actors. The overwhelming majority of the population which is apparently hostile, or at best hesitant, can only be won over for the European cause if the project is rescued from the pallid abstractions of administrative measures and technical discourse; in other words, the project must be politicized. The intellectuals have dropped the ball, and the politicians are even less eager to get their fingers burnt on such an unpopular cause. All the more noteworthy, therefore, is the stimulus given to a constitutional debate by Joschka Fischer's speech at the Humboldt University on May 12, 2000.[28] Fischer's question – how can we construct the right kind of relation between the "Europe of states" and the "Europe of citizens"? – has prompted Chirac, Prodi, Rau, and Schröder to respond with their own proposals. But it was Jospin who pointed out that no reform of procedures and institutions can succeed until the content of the underlying political project has taken on sharper contours.

The decidedly nationalist orientation of the Bush administration can also be regarded as an opportunity for the EU to develop a more distinctive common foreign and security policy with regard to the conflicts in the Middle East and the Balkans and relations with Russia and China. Policy differences over the environment, military procurement, and law which are emerging more clearly are contributing to a silent strengthening of European identity. Still more important is the question of what role Europe wishes to play in the Security Council and, above all, in global economic institutions. Contrasting justifications for humanitarian interventions, and above all fundamental differences in economic policy, presage the fault lines dividing the EU founding states from Great Britain and the Scandinavian countries. But it is better to bring these smoldering conflicts out into the open than to let the Union fracture under the weight of unresolved dilemmas. In any case, a Europe of two or three speeds is preferable to one which collapses or slowly disintegrates.

Jospin's hint at what the "mechanism for strengthened cooperation" agreed at the Nice conference might mean was unmistakable: "It could certainly be applied to the coordination of economic policy in the Euro-zone, but also in fields like public health and military procurement. Through these forms of cooperation, a group of states could once again give the construction of Europe the impetus which it has always needed." A sober interest calculation could well induce the French and German governments to seize the initiative again following the upcoming elections to the Elysée and the Bundestag. As the *International Herald Tribune* dryly remarked: "In the last resort, the French will be prepared to pay a certain price for Berlin not becoming the capital of Europe" (June 12, 2001). In line with the foreign policy of Genscher and Fischer, we would be well advised to agree with this. Since diplomacy is at an impasse, the long-overdue institutional reform can only benefit from an open political debate over the direction in which the EU should develop. The constitutional dispute between the "federalists" and "sovereignists" only serves to mask the substantive conflict between those who see a pressing need for harmonization of major national policies, on the one hand, and those who would like to see a façade of tailor-made central institutions stripped of all important regulatory functions, on the other. All sides rightly regard the division of competences between the federal, national, and regional levels as the core political issue to be settled by the organizational clauses of the constitution. They also agree that the historical nation-states must retain a substantially stronger status than would normally be enjoyed by the constituent parts of a federal state. The at present still dominant role of compromise-formation between states will also remain pronounced, though subject to constitutional controls.[29]

Hence, a Chamber of Nationalities that would lend the European Council the status of a permanent senate would not only function as a legislative body in competition and cooperation with the European Parliament, but would also retain direct access to the European Commission, which would in turn develop into a politically legitimate executive branch. The two authorities together would perform approximately the functions of government exercised by a strong presidency, in a complementary relation to a parliament directly elected in accordance with a uniform electoral law. Given this division of powers and the likelihood of a weak party system at the European level, the European Parliament would have a similar status to the American Congress in certain respects. And the European Court of Justice, as the institution responsible for elaborating law, would also gain greater influence and perhaps acquire a status similar to that of the US Supreme Court. For the enormous increase in the complexity of the matters in need of regulation calls for detailed constitutional interpretations designed to reduce the proliferation of international treaties to abstract principles.[30]

I would like to offer three reflections on the wide-ranging debate over legal procedures.

First, the political substance of a future European constitution would consist in a definitive answer to the question of the territorial boundaries of the European Union, coupled with a less-than-definitive answer to the question of how competences are to be divided within a multilevel political system. The determination of definitive frontiers is compatible with the "variable geometry" of a more or less accelerated integration of member states. A "Europe of different speeds," temporarily differentiated into center and periphery, could also alleviate the problems associated with the eastward enlargement. The controversial division of competences should be resolved immediately, but in a way that remains open for future revisions. This will allow for experimentation while leaving room for learning from unforeseen consequences within a stable framework. Moreover, such a temporalization of specific, albeit central, constitutional requirements is compatible with a dynamic understanding of the democratic constitution as an ever more exhaustive realization of a system of basic rights.[31]

Second, "subsidiarity" is the often-invoked functional principle for safeguarding the independence of the member nation-states. Of course, the greater the differences in territory, size of population, political power, level of economic development, culture, and lifestyles, the greater the danger that majority decisions will violate the principle of coexistence among equals. Therefore, all matters which are sensitive for the preservation of national integrity must be screened from majoritarian decisions. In consensus-based democracies organized around social "pillars," however, political decisions notoriously suffer from a lack of transparency. Therefore, we should consider pan-European referenda as a way of enhancing citizens' opportunities to influence the shaping of policy.[32]

Third, both Fischer and Jospin have taken up the idea of establishing horizontal links between national parliaments. The proposal is to address the democratic deficit by dovetailing the respective national parliaments in a way which mirrors the association of governments in the European Council. The chain of legitimacy running through the European Parliament would be strengthened if either a portion of the members of the European Parliament were simultaneously members of their respective national parliaments, or if the largely neglected Conference of European Affairs Committee were to revive the practice of horizontal exchanges between the national parliaments.[33] Other considerations bring alternative routes of legitimation into play. The approach known as "comitology," for example, ascribes the legitimating role of deliberative politics to the large number of advisory committees which support the work of the European Commission.[34]

Part V

A Question of Political Theory

The question of the relation between popular sovereignty and human rights is answered quite differently in the liberal and the republican traditions. The friendly criticisms of the constitutional theorist Frank Michelman, who teaches at the Harvard Law School, provide an opportunity for a further attempt to present as clearly as possible the basic idea of my book *Between Facts and Norms*, namely, an explanation of the co-originality of democracy and the rule of law in terms of the theory of discourse.

8

Constitutional Democracy – A Paradoxical Union of Contradictory Principles?[1]

The modern conception of democracy differs from the classical conception in virtue of its relation to a type of law that displays three characteristics: modern law is positive, compulsory, and individualistic. Such law consists of norms that are produced by a lawgiver, are sanctioned by the state, and are meant to guarantee individual liberties. According to the liberal view, the democratic self-determination of citizens can be realized only through the medium of such a law, the structural properties of which ensure liberty. Consequently, the idea of a "rule of law," which in the past was expressed in the idea of human rights, comes on the scene alongside – and together with – that of popular sovereignty as a second source of legitimation. This duality raises the question of how the democratic principle and constitutionalism are related.[2]

According to the classical conception, the laws of a republic express the *unrestricted* will of the united citizens. Regardless of how the laws reflect the existing ethos of the shared political life, this ethos presents no limitation insofar as it achieves its validity only through the citizens' own process of will-formation. The principle of the constitutional exercise of power, on the other hand, appears to set limits on the people's sovereign self-determination. The rule of law requires that democratic will-formation does not violate human rights that have been positively enacted as basic rights. The two sources of legitimation also compete with each other in the history of political philosophy. Liberalism and civic republicanism disagree on whether the "liberty of the moderns" or the "liberty of the ancients" should enjoy priority in the order of justification. Which comes first? The individual liberties of the members of the modern market society or the rights of democratic citizens to political participation?

The one side insists that, in basic rights, the private autonomy of citizens assumes a form that – "unchangeable" in its essential content – guarantees the anonymous rule of law. According to the other side, the political autonomy of citizens is embodied in the self-organization of a community that freely makes its own laws. If the normative justification of constitutional democracy is to be consistent, then it seems one must rank the two principles, human rights and popular sovereignty. To be legitimate, laws, including basic rights, must either agree with human rights (however these in turn are legitimated), or they must issue from democratic will-formation. On the first alternative, the democratic lawgiver may decide in a sovereign manner only within the boundaries of human rights; on the second alternative, the democratic lawgiver can set up any constitution it wants and, as the case may be, violate its own basic law, thus impairing the idea of the constitutional state.

However, these alternatives contradict a strong intuition.[3] The idea of human rights that is spelled out in basic rights may neither be imposed on the sovereign lawgiver as a limitation nor be merely instrumentalized as a functional requisite for legislative purposes. In a certain way, we consider both principles as equally original. One is not possible without the other, but neither sets limits on the other. The intuition of "co-originality" can also be expressed thus: private and public autonomy require each other. The two concepts are interdependent; they are related to each other by material implication. Citizens can make an *appropriate* use of their public autonomy, as guaranteed by political rights, only if they are sufficiently independent in virtue of an equally protected private autonomy in their life conduct. But members of society actually enjoy their equal private autonomy to an equal extent – that is, equally distributed individual liberties have "equal value" for them – only if as citizens they make an appropriate use of their political autonomy.

Rousseau and Kant formulated this intuition in the concept of autonomy.[4] The idea that the addressees of the law must also be able to understand themselves as its authors does not give the united citizens of a democratic polity a voluntaristic, *carte blanche* permission to make whatever decisions they like. The legal guarantee to behave as one pleases within the bounds of the law is the core of private, not public, autonomy. Rather, on the basis of this freedom of choice, citizens are accorded autonomy in the sense of a *reasonable* will-formation, even if this autonomy can only be enjoined [*angesonnen*] and not legally required of them. They should bind their wills to just those laws they give themselves after achieving a common will through discourse. Correctly understood, the idea of self-legislation engenders an internal relation between will and reason in such a way that the freedom of everyone – that is, self-legislation – depends on the *equal* consideration of the individual freedom of each individual to take a yes/no position – that is, self-*legislation*. Under these conditions, only those laws that lie in the equal interest of each can meet with the reasonable agreement of all.

However, neither Rousseau nor Kant could find an unambiguous way of using the concept of autonomy for the justification of constitutional democracy. Rousseau inscribed the will of the people with reason by binding the democratic process to the abstract and universal form of laws, whereas Kant tried to accomplish this relation to reason by subordinating law to morality. As I will show, however, this internal connection between will and reason can develop only in the dimension of time – as a self-correcting historical process.

It is true, of course, that, in the *Conflict of the Faculties*, Kant went beyond the systematic boundaries of his own philosophy and raised the French Revolution to the level of a "historical sign" for the possibility of a moral progress of humanity.[5] But in the theory itself we find no trace of the constitutional assemblies of Philadelphia and Paris – at least not the reasonable trace of a great, dual historical event that we can now see in retrospect as an entirely new beginning. With this event began a project that holds together a rational constitutional discourse across the centuries. In what follows, I take a recent study by Frank Michelman[6] as the occasion to argue that the allegedly paradoxical relation between democracy and the rule of law resolves itself in the dimension of historical time, provided one conceives the constitution as a project that makes the founding act into an ongoing process of constitution-making that continues across generations.

Political systems such as the United States and the German Federal Republic have set up an independent institution charged with scrutinizing the constitutionality of parliamentary legislation. In these settings, the function and status of this politically influential branch

– the Federal Constitutional Court or Supreme Court – spark debates over the relation between democracy and the rule of law. In the United States, a debate has been going on for some time over the legitimacy of the highest-level judicial review exercised by the Supreme Court. Again and again, civic republicans who are convinced that "all government is by the people" bristle at the elite power of legal experts to void the decisions of a democratically elected legislature, although these experts themselves are not legitimated by a democratic majority but can only call upon their technical competence in constitutional interpretation. Frank Michelman sees this problematic personified in William J. Brennan, a commanding figure in recent American constitutional jurisprudence. As Michelman describes him, Brennan is a liberal who defends individual liberties in strongly moralistic terms; a democrat who radicalizes rights of political participation and wants to give a hearing to the voiceless and marginalized as well as to the deviant and oppositional voices; a social democrat who is highly sensitive to questions of social justice; and, finally, a pluralist who, going beyond the liberal understanding of tolerance, pleads for a politics open to difference and to the recognition of cultural, racial, and religious minorities. In short, by employing the palette of American pragmatism to depict Brennan as a model of contemporary republicanism, Michelman wants to sharpen the question that interests us here: when a convinced democrat with this mentality, in the role of a highly activist Supreme Court judge, has no qualms in making extensive use of the dubious instrument of judicial oversight, then perhaps the jurisprudence he has shaped reveals the secret of how one can combine the principle of popular sovereignty with constitutionalism.

Michelman uses Brennan to exemplify the role of a "responsive judge" who qualifies as *democratically above suspicion* when it comes to interpreting the Constitution. Brennan qualifies for this trust because he renders his decisions as best he knows how and according to his conscience and only after he has listened as patiently as possible – with an inquisitive hermeneutic sensitivity and a desire to learn – to the tangle of views in the relevant discourses conducted in civil society and the political public sphere. Interaction with the larger public, before whom legal experts are held responsible, is supposed to contribute to the democratic legitimation of the decisions of a constitutional judge who has not been democratically legitimated, or at least not sufficiently legitimated:

It is a condition of the interpreter's greater or lesser reliability *and of what we can do to bolster it*. And one condition that you think contributes greatly to reliability is the constant exposure of the interpreter – the moral reader – to the full blast of the sundry opinions on the questions of rightness of one or another interpretation, freely and uninhibitedly produced by assorted members of society listening to what the others have to say out of their diverse life histories, current situations, and perceptions of interest and need.[7]

Michelman is apparently guided by the intuition that the discursive besiegement of the Court by a mobilized society gives rise to an interaction that has favorable consequences for both sides. For the Court, which as always decides independently, the perspective of the experts is broadened along with the base of justifications for its decision. For citizens, whose provocative public opinions exert an influence on the Court, the legitimacy of the decision procedure is at least increased. To judge how this model can help resolve the alleged paradox, one would have to analyze in detail, on the one hand, the cognitive role played by the discursive offensive as a means of broadening the legal public sphere for the practice of the Court and, on the other, the functional contribution such discourse is supposed to have for the social acceptance of the decision. However, I suspect that pragmatic reasons and historical circumstances are more decisive for determining how the task of judicial oversight is best *established* in a given context. These institutional possibilities should certainly be assessed in the light of the principles of popular sovereignty and constitutionalism, but the constellation and interplay of these principles do not yield pat answers.

For our main issue, I find the *way* Michelman arrives at his model of the "responsive" judge more interesting than the proposal itself. For some time now, Michelman has debated against essentially three positions (which he sees represented by Ronald Dworkin, Robert Post, and myself).[8] In what follows, I stylize the arguments and counterarguments in such a way that these three positions "emerge from one another" in good dialectical fashion.

According to the liberal view, the democratic legislative process requires a specific form of legal institutionalization if it is to lead to legitimate regulations. A "basic law" is introduced as the necessary and sufficient condition for the democratic process itself, not for its results: democracy cannot define democracy. The relationship between democracy as the source of legitimation and a constitutionalism that does not need democratic legitimation poses no paradox, however. For constitutive rules that first *make a democracy possible* cannot *constrain* democratic practice in the manner of externally imposed norms. By simply clarifying the concepts, the alleged paradox disappears: enabling conditions should not be confused with constraining conditions.

The conclusion that the constitution is in some sense inherent in democracy is certainly plausible. But the argument put forth as justification is inadequate because it refers only to part of the basic law, the part immediately constitutive for institutions of opinion- and will-formation – that is, it refers only to rights of political participation and communication. But liberty rights make up the core of basic rights – habeas corpus, freedom of religion, property rights – in short, all those liberties that guarantee an autonomous life-conduct and the pursuit of happiness. These liberal basic rights evidently protect goods that also have an *intrinsic* value. They cannot be reduced to the instrumental function they can have for the exercise of the political rights of citizens. Because the classical liberties are not primarily intended to foster the qualification for political citizenship, liberal rights, unlike political rights, cannot be justified by the argument that they make democracy possible.

According to the republican view, the substance of the constitution will not compete with the sovereignty of the people if the constitution itself emerges from an inclusive process of opinion- and will-formation on the part of citizens. To be sure, we must then conceive democratic self-determination as an uncoerced process of ethical-political self-understanding undertaken by a populace accustomed to freedom. Under these conditions the rule of law remains unharmed because it gains recognition as an integral component of a *democratic ethos*. Rooted in the motivations and attitudes of the citizens, constitutional principles are less coercive and more permanent than formal juridical mechanisms that immunize the constitution against changes by tyrannical majorities. However, this reflection is guilty of begging the question; that is, it builds into the history of ideas and political culture of the polity precisely those liberal value-orientations that make legal coercion superfluous by replacing it with custom and moral self-control.

The republican conception acquires a different, namely proceduralist, sense when the expectation of reason connected with a *self-*

limiting democratic opinion- and will-formation shifts from a basis in the resources of an existing value consensus to the formal properties of the democratic process. Neo-Aristotelians must bank on the liberal quality and tradition-building force of a democratic form of life; neo-Kantians, by contrast, radicalize the view that the idea of human rights is inherent in the very process of a reasonable will-formation: basic rights are answers that meet the demands of a political communication among strangers and ground the presumption that outcomes are rationally acceptable. The constitution thereby acquires the procedural sense of establishing forms of communication that provide for the public use of reason and a fair balance of interests in a manner consonant with the regulatory need and context-specific issue. Because this ensemble of enabling conditions must be realized in the medium of law, these rights encompass both liberal freedoms and rights of political participation, as we shall see.

It is not without sympathy that Michelman describes the basic assumptions of this conception of deliberative democracy:

> [F]irst, a belief that only in the wake of democratic debate can anyone hope to arrive at a reliable approximation to true answers to questions of justice of proposed constitutional norms, understood as consisting in their universalizability of everyone's interests or their hypothetical unanimous acceptability in a democratic discourse; and, second, that only in that way can anyone hope to gain a sufficient grasp of relevant historical conditions to produce for the country in question, in a legally workable form, an apt interpretation of whatever abstract practical norms can pass the justice tests of universalizability and democratic-discursive acceptability.[9]

However, Michelman does not regard this conception of deliberative democracy as a solution to the supposedly paradoxical relation between democracy and the rule of law. The paradox seems to return when we trace matters back to the act of constitution-making and ask whether discourse theory allows us to conceive the opinion- and will-formation of the constitutional convention as an unconstrained democratic process. Elsewhere, I have proposed that we understand the normative bases of constitutional democracy as the result of a deliberative decision-making process that the founders – motivated by whatever historical contingencies – undertook with the intention of creating a voluntary, self-determining association of free and equal citizens.[10] The founders sought a reasonable answer to this question:

what rights must we mutually accord one another if we want legitimately to regulate our common life by means of positive law?

Given this way of framing the issue and given a discursive mode of deliberation, two things follow. First, only those outcomes can count as legitimate upon which equally entitled participants in the deliberation can freely agree – that is, outcomes that meet with the justified consent of all under conditions of rational discourse. Second, given the specific way of framing the question, the participants commit themselves to modern law as the medium for regulating their common life. The mode of legitimation through a general consent under discursive conditions realizes the Kantian concept of political autonomy only in connection with the idea of coercive laws that grant equal individual liberties. For, according to the Kantian concept of autonomy, no one is truly free until all citizens enjoy equal liberties under laws that they have given themselves after a reasonable deliberation.

Before I recall the system of rights that emerges from this discourse-theoretic approach, I must deal with the objection Michelman raises against this third, proceduralist attempt at reconciling the idea of human rights with the principle of popular sovereignty. To perceive the force of this interesting objection, one must be clear about the consequences of attempting to explain the form of constitutional democracy in terms of the *legal institutionalization* of a far-reaching network of discourses. Public discourses must be temporally, socially, and materially specified in relation to political opinion- and will-formation in arenas of the public sphere or in legislative bodies and in relation to legally correct and materially informed decision-making practices in courts or administrations. Michelman has in view this dimension of legal regulations, beginning with basic rights and voting rights, extending further to the specifications of the organizational part of the constitution, and finally moving to the procedural rights and rules of order of individual governmental bodies.

Depending on the matter in need of regulation and the need for a decision, sometimes the moral and legal aspects of an issue stand in the foreground; at other times the ethical aspects stand out. Sometimes empirical questions are involved that call for expert knowledge; at other times it is a matter of pragmatic questions that require a balancing of interests and, thus, fair negotiations. The legitimation processes themselves move through various levels of communication. Standing in contrast to the "wild" circuits of communication in the unorganized public sphere are the formally regulated deliberative and decision-making processes of courts, parliaments, bureaucracies, and the like. The legal procedures and norms that govern institutional-ized discourses should not be confused with the cognitive procedures and patterns of argumentation that guide the intrinsic course of discourse itself.

It is this legal dimension of the process of establishing forms of communication that Michelman refers to when he argues that the constitution-making practice cannot be reconstructed on the basis of discourse theory. The reason is that this approach cannot avoid the circularity of legal self-constitution and thus gets trapped in an infinite regress:

> A truly democratic process is itself inescapably a legally conditioned and constituted process. It is constituted, for example, by laws regard-ing political representation and elections, civil associations, families, freedom of speech, property, access to media, and so on. Thus, in order to confer legitimacy on a set of laws issuing from an actual set of dis-cursive institutions and practices in a country, those institutions and practices would themselves have to be legally constituted in the right way. The laws regarding elections, representation, associations, fami-lies, speech, property, and so on, would have to be such as to consti-tute a process of more or less "fair" or "undistorted" democratic political communication, not only in the formal arenas of legislation and adju-dication but in civil society at large. The problem is that whether they do or not may itself at any time become a matter of contentious but reasonable disagreement, according to the liberal premise of reason-able interpretative pluralism.[11]

The procedural legitimacy of the outcome of any given discourse depends on the legitimacy of the rules according to which that type of discourse has been specified and established from temporal, social, and material points of view. If procedural legitimacy is the standard, then the outcome of political elections, the decision of parliaments, or the content of court decisions are in principle subject to the sus-picion that they came about in the wrong way, according to deficient rules and in a deficient institutional framework. This chain of pre-suppositions of legitimation reaches back even beyond the constitu-tion-making practice. For example, the constitutional assembly cannot itself vouch for the legitimacy of the rules according to which it was constituted. The chain never terminates, and the democratic process is caught in a circular self-constitution that leads to an infinite regress.

I prefer not to meet this objection by recourse to the dubious objectivity of ultimate moral insights that are supposed to bring the regress to a halt. Rather than appeal to a moral realism that would be hard to defend, I propose that we understand the regress itself as the understandable expression of the future-oriented character, or openness, of the democratic constitution: in my view, a constitution that is democratic – not just in its content but also according to its source of legitimation – is a tradition-building project with a clearly marked beginning in time. All the later generations have the task of actualizing the still-untapped normative substance of the system of rights laid down in the original document of the constitution. According to this dynamic understanding of the constitution, ongoing legislation carries on the system of rights by interpreting and adapting them for current circumstances (and to this extent, levels off the threshold between constitutional norms and ordinary law). To be sure, this fallible continuation of the founding event can break out of the circle of a polity's groundless discursive self-constitution only if this process – which is not immune to contingent interruptions and historical regressions – can be understood in the long run as a self-correcting learning process.

In a country such as the United States, which can look back on more than 200 years of continuous constitutional history, we find evidence that supports this dynamic interpretation. Bruce Ackerman refers to "hot" periods, such as the New Deal under Roosevelt, that were characterized by the innovative spirit of successful reforms. Such times of productive radical change make possible the rare experience of emancipation and leave behind the memory of an instructive historical example. Contemporaries can see that groups hitherto discriminated against gain their own voice and that hitherto underprivileged classes are put into a position to take their fate into their own hands. Once the interpretive battles have subsided, all parties recognize that the reforms are achievements, although they were at first sharply contested. In retrospect they agree that, with the inclusion of marginalized groups and with the empowerment of deprived classes, the hitherto poorly satisfied presuppositions for the legitimacy of existing democratic procedures are better realized.

Of course, the interpretation of constitutional history as a learning process is predicated on the non-trivial assumption that later generations will start with the same standards as did the founders. Whoever bases her judgment today on the normative expectation of complete inclusion and mutual recognition, as well as on the expectation of equal opportunities for utilizing equal rights, must assume that she can find these standards by reasonably appropriating the constitution and its history of interpretation. The descendants can learn from past mistakes only if they are "in the same boat" as their forebears. They must impute to all the previous generations the same intention of creating and expanding the bases for a voluntary association of citizens who make their own laws. All participants must be able to recognize the project as *the same* throughout history and to judge it from the same perspective.

Michelman seems to agree:

> Constitutional framers can be *our* framers – their history can be our history, their word can command observance from us now on popular sovereignty grounds – only because and insofar as they, in our eyes now, were already on what we judge to be the track of true constitutional reason. . . . In the production of present-day legal authority, constitutional framers have to be figures of rightness for us before they can be figures of history.[12]

The unifying bond thus consists of the *shared* practice to which we have recourse when we endeavor to arrive at a rational understanding of the text of the constitution. It is no accident that the founding constitutional act is experienced as a decisive point in the nation's history, because with this act the grounds for a world-historically new kind of practice have been established. The performative meaning of this practice – a practice meant to bring forth a self-determining community of free and equal citizens – is simply spelled out in the words of the constitution. This meaning remains dependent on an ongoing explication that is carried out in the course of applying, interpreting, and supplementing constitutional norms.

Thanks to this intuitively available performative meaning, each citizen of a democratic polity can at any time refer to the texts and decisions of the founders and their descendants in a critical fashion, just as one can, conversely, adopt the perspective of the founders and take a critical view of the present to test whether the existing institutions, practices, and procedures of democratic opinion- and will-formation satisfy the necessary conditions for a process that engenders legitimacy. Philosophers and other experts can in their own way contribute explanations of what it means to pursue the project of realizing a self-determining association of free and equal consociates under law. On this premise, each founding act also creates the possibility of a process of self-correcting attempts to tap the system of rights ever more fully.

Reflection on the historical dimension of realizing the constitutional project can, perhaps, defang the prima facie plausible objection to the discourse-theoretic interpretation of the democratic self-constitution of the constitutional state [*Verfassungsstaat*]. But one has not thereby shown how the principles of the rule of law found in the constitution are inherent in democracy itself. To demonstrate that democracy and constitutionalism are not paradoxically related, we must explain the sense in which basic rights *as a whole*, and not merely political rights, are constitutive for the process of self-legislation.

Similar to its social-contract predecessors, discourse theory simulates an original condition: an arbitrary number of persons freely enter into a constitution-making practice. The fiction of freedom satisfies the important condition of an original equality of the participating parties, whose "yes" and "no" count equally. The participants must satisfy three further conditions. First, they are united by a common resolution to regulate their future life together legitimately by means of positive law. Second, they are ready and able to take part in rational discourses and thus to satisfy the demanding pragmatic presuppositions of a practice of argumentation. Unlike the tradition of modern natural law, this supposition of rationality is not limited to purposive rationality; moreover, in contrast to Rousseau and Kant it does not just extend to morality but makes communicative reason a condition.[13] Finally, entrance into the practice of constitution-making is bound up with the readiness to make the meaning of this practice an explicit topic (i.e., to make the resources of the performance a topic of discussion). That is, to begin with, the practice amounts to nothing more than reflecting on and conceptually explicating the specific meaning of the intended enterprise on which the participants have embarked with their very practice of constitution-making. This reflection attends to a series of constructive tasks that must be com-

pleted before the work of constitution-making can actually begin –
the next stage.

The first thing the participants recognize is that, because they want
to realize their intention through the medium of law, they must
create a system of statuses that ensures that every future member of
the association counts as a bearer of individual rights. A system of
positive and compulsory law with such an individualistic quality can
come about only if three categories of rights are concomitantly introduced. If we consider that the capacity for general consent is a
requirement of legitimacy, these categories are as follows:

- basic rights (whatever their concrete content) that result from the
  autonomous elaboration of the right to the greatest possible
  measure of equal individual freedom of action for each person;
- basic rights (whatever their concrete content) that result from the
  autonomous elaboration of the status of a member in a voluntary
  association of legal consociates;
- basic rights (whatever their concrete content) that result from the
  autonomous elaboration of each individual's right to equal
  protection under law, that is, that result from the actionability of
  individual rights.

These three categories of rights are the necessary basis for an association of citizens that has definite social boundaries and whose
members mutually recognize one another as bearers of actionable
individual rights.

In respect to the above three categories, however, participants
anticipate only that they will be future users and *addressees* of the
law. Because they want to ground an association of citizens who make
their own laws, it next occurs to them that they need a fourth category of rights so that they can mutually recognize one another also
as the *authors* of these rights as well as of the law in general. If they
want to hold fast to the most important aspect of their practice, its
self-determining character, not only now but also in the future, then
they must empower themselves as political lawgivers by introducing
basic political rights. Without the first three categories of basic rights,
something like law cannot exist; but without a political elaboration
of these categories the law could not acquire any concrete contents.
For the latter, an additional (and also initially empty) category of
rights is necessary:

- basic rights (whatever their concrete content) that emerge from the autonomous elaboration of the right to an equal opportunity to participate in political law-giving.

It is important to keep in mind that this scenario has recapitulated a thought process carried out *in mente*, so to speak – even if the process is supposed to have taken shape in the course of a deliberative practice. Thus far, nothing has *actually* happened. Nothing could happen: before the participants conclude their first act of lawmaking, they must achieve clarity regarding the enterprise they have resolved upon with their entrance into a practice of constitution-making. However, after they have made explicit their intuitive knowledge of the performative meaning of this practice, they know they must create the four above categories of basic rights in a single stroke, so to speak. Of course, they cannot produce basic rights *in abstracto* but only particular basic rights with a concrete content. For this reason, the participants who thus far were engaged in inward reflection, focused on a kind of philosophical clarification, must step out from behind the veil of empirical ignorance and perceive what in general must be regulated under the given historical circumstances and which rights are necessary for dealing with these matters in need of regulation.

Only when they are confronted, we say, with the intolerable consequences of the use of physical violence do they recognize the necessity of elementary rights to bodily integrity or to freedom of movement. The constitutional assembly can reach decisions only when they see the risks that make a specific need for security into a matter they must address. Only the introduction of new information technologies leads to problems that make some kind of data protection necessary. Only when the relevant features of the environment shed light on our own interests does it become clear that we need rights that protect the conduct of our personal and political life – such familiar rights as the right to conclude contracts and acquire property, to form associations and publicly express our opinions, to join and practice a religion, and so on.

We must, therefore, carefully distinguish two stages. The first stage involves the conceptual explication of the language of individual rights in which the shared practice of a self-determining association of free and equal citizens can express itself – thus, rights in which alone the principle of popular sovereignty can be embodied. The second stage involves the realization of this principle through the exercise, the actual carrying out, of this practice. Because the practice of civic self-determination is conceived as a long-run process of realizing and progressively elaborating the system of fundamental rights, the principle of popular sovereignty comes into its own as part and parcel of the idea of government by law. This two-stage scenario of the conceptual genesis of basic rights clearly shows that the preparatory conceptual steps explicate necessary requirements for a legally established democratic self-legislation. They express this practice itself and are not constraints to which the practice would be subjected. Only together with the idea of government by law can the democratic principle be realized. The two principles stand in a reciprocal relationship of material implication.

Because autonomy must not be confused with arbitrary freedom of choice, the rule of law neither precedes the will of the sovereign nor issues from that will. Rather, the rule of law is inscribed in political self-legislation, just as the categorical imperative – the idea that only universalizable maxims, maxims capable of universal consent, are legitimate and reasonable in the sense of showing equal respect for each person – is inscribed in moral self-legislation. However, whereas the morally acting individual binds her will to the idea of *justice*, the reasonable self-binding of the political sovereign means that the latter binds itself to legitimate *law*. The practical reason that is articulated in the rule of law is, as legally exercised rulership, bound up with the constitutive features of modern law. This explains why the co-implication of popular sovereignty and constitutionalism is reflected in the relation between the autonomy of the citizen and the autonomy of the private individual: one cannot be realized without the other.

Like morality, so also legitimate law protects the equal autonomy of each person: no individual is free so long as all persons do not enjoy an equal freedom. But the positivity of law necessitates an interesting split in autonomy to which there is nothing analogous in the moral sphere. The binding character of legal norms stems not just from the insight into what is equally good for all, but from the collectively binding decisions of authorities who make and apply the law. This results in the conceptually necessary division of roles between authors who make and apply the law, on the one hand, and addressees who are subject to valid law, on the other. The autonomy that in the moral sphere springs from a single source, as it were, appears in the legal sphere in the dual form of private and public autonomy.

Modern compulsory law can demand only that its addressees behave in a legal manner: that regardless of one's motivation, one behave in conformity with law. Because the law may not require legal obedience "out of respect for the law," private autonomy can be guaranteed only in the form of individual liberties that entitle one to an autonomous life-conduct and enable the moral consideration of others but do not obligate one to do anything beyond what is compatible with the equal freedom of everyone else. Private autonomy thus takes on the form of a legally guaranteed freedom of choice. At the same time, in the role of persons who act morally, legal persons must also be able to follow the law out of respect for the law. For this reason, valid (in the sense of existing) law must also be legitimate. And the law can satisfy this condition only if it has come about in a legitimate way, namely, according to the procedures of democratic opinion- and will-formation that justify the presumption that outcomes are rationally acceptable. The entitlement to political participation is bound up with the expectation of a public use of reason: as democratic co-legislators, citizens may not ignore the informal demand [*Ansinnen*] to orient themselves toward the common good.

The foregoing makes it appear as if practical reason has its place only in the exercise of a political autonomy that allows the addressees of law to understand themselves simultaneously as its authors. In fact, practical reason is realized in the form of private autonomy no less than it is in that of political autonomy. That is, both are as much means for the other as they are ends in themselves. The demand to orient oneself to the common good, which is connected with political autonomy, is also a rational expectation insofar as only the democratic process guarantees that private individuals will achieve an equal enjoyment of their equal individual liberties. Conversely, only when the private autonomy of individuals is secure are citizens in a position to make correct use of their political autonomy. The interdependence of constitutionalism and democracy comes to light in this complementary relationship between private and civic autonomy: each side is fed by resources it has from the other.

Part VI

American Pragmatism and German Philosophy: Three Reviews

The translations of a classic work by John Dewey from 1929, of a patriotic treatise by my friend Richard Rorty, and of a groundbreaking new work by Robert Brandom led me to reflect (in *Die Zeit*, July 23, 1998, the *Süddeutsche Zeitung*, February 27–28, 1999, and the *Frankfurter Rundschau*, June 20, 2000, respectively) on the strangely belated but now widespread reception that pragmatism has experienced in Germany.

9

John Dewey, *The Quest for Certainty*

If we cast a retrospective glance over the twentieth century, then the 1920s emerge as the most fruitful decade for German philosophy, with the publication of Wittgenstein's *Tractatus*, Lukács' *History and Class Consciousness*, Cassirer's *Philosophy of Symbolic Forms*, Scheler's *The Forms of Knowledge and Society*, Plessner's *The Stages of the Organic and Man*, and, of course, Heidegger's *Being and Time*. Shortly thereafter, in 1929, a book of comparable importance appeared in the United States, *The Quest for Certainty*, the most influential work of John Dewey who was then at the height of his fame at the age of 70. It has taken a long time for this classic of American pragmatism to appear in a German translation by Martin Suhr.[1] These days there is much talk of Dewey. Even in Germany, "pragmatism" has changed from an insult into a compliment. Nevertheless, Dewey's belated reception reminds us of the asymmetrical relationship between Dewey and his German counterparts.

As a college student in his native city of Burlington, Vermont, a stronghold of transcendentalism, Dewey had already familiarized himself with Kant, Fichte, Schelling, and Hegel. But the seed of his own "naturalized" Hegelianism only later took root in the home of German idealism. It was not until a decade or more after the end of World War II that pragmatism began to be taken seriously in Germany as a long-overlooked variant of young Hegelianism and a source of related philosophical themes. As we can see from the publication dates of translations, even this process of assimilation in the early 1960s initially focused more narrowly on Charles Saunders Peirce and George Herbert Mead than on Dewey and William James.

Today, pragmatism in all its variants forms a transatlantic bridge for a lively philosophical exchange in both directions. Anyone who reads *The Quest for Certainty* with its historical reception in mind will discover in the book itself the reasons for the tensions and misunderstandings between Dewey and the three philosophical traditions in Germany which, albeit in different ways, were closest to him.

Dewey focuses on everyday practices in which people must "grapple" and "come to terms" with reality. Here, the category of "action" takes on an unprecedented philosophical importance. Informed by the philosophy of history, Dewey directs his attention primarily at the interface between knowledge and action with the aim of assigning philosophy a new task. He advocates reversing classical theory's flight from the world and a return to practical engagement with reality. Science and technology are ceaselessly accelerating the mastery of nature and industrial development, thereby showing how knowledge can become practical because it is inherently oriented to practice. By contrast, politics and education, the promotion of civility and the cultivation of taste, and, in general, the self-organization of society are in a parlous state because a comparably intelligent form of guidance is lacking. Philosophy has failed to provide it. Instead of policing the gap between the higher and the lower, philosophy should renounce the supposed certainty of pure theory. It must face up to the challenges of a contingent world and enter into cooperation with the sciences, instead of adopting a fundamentalist attitude toward them. Only in this way can it open up secure horizons of possibility for the "forms of social and personal action." With this revolution in the self-understanding of philosophy, Dewey positioned himself between all the stools. His opposition to the logical empiricism of Carnap and Reichenbach is no less pronounced than the contrast with the philosophical idealism of Scheler and Heidegger and the anti-scientism of Horkheimer and Adorno. During the 1930s in the United States, Dewey's philosophy was already to a certain extent being displaced by the analytic philosophy of science professed by the thinkers who had been driven out of Austria and Germany. These emigrants certainly had great sympathy with the "scientific spirit" which they encountered in pragmatist circles and sought the collaboration of Dewey with their project of unified science. But when the 80-year-old Dewey was honored with the first volume of the now-famous

"Library of Living Philosophers" in 1939, the voices of the empiricists, as Hans Reichenbach's contribution shows, were already quite critical.

There were two essential differences between them. On the one hand, in *The Quest for Certainty*, Dewey criticizes the empiricist "spectator model of knowledge" according to which elementary sensations provide a secure basis of experience. We have experiences only through our active dealings with a reality that can contradict the expectations that guide action. Hence reality does not disclose itself through the receptivity of the senses but in a constructive manner, in the performance of actions. We do not "grasp" objects independently of the controlled success of deliberately executed actions. This is the point of scientific experiments. On the other hand, Dewey criticizes empiricist moral theories which trace value judgments back to emotions, impulses, or decisions. Dewey is committed to the view that value judgments have cognitive content. On his account, "judgments about desirable and praiseworthy matters" acquire objectivity insofar as they are connected with knowledge of the conditions of success of a practice through which we can achieve corresponding goals.

With these reflections, Dewey was not able to satisfy the need for explanations which had developed among the younger generation. In the leading American university departments he remained a "has-been." This situation only began to change in 1979 when Richard Rorty placed Dewey alongside Wittgenstein and Heidegger as "one of the three most significant philosophers of our century." Unlike in the United States, however, in Germany Dewey had not even had an earlier reception, apart, that is, from pedagogy and Gehlen's anthropology. Max Scheler had indeed assimilated important pragmatist themes in his sociology of knowledge; but he remained committed to a hierarchy of forms of knowledge according to which "mastering" or "controlling" knowledge [*Herrschafts oder Leistungswissen*] – the only kind that Dewey allowed – remained subordinated to "cultural" and "redemptive" forms of knowledge. Scheler himself is an example of a kind of Platonism that satisfies the quest for certainty through a metaphysical surrogate, the flight into the realm of ideas. Idealism elevates contemplation to the path to philosophical salvation. In Dewey's view, it thereby misses the path to the only kind of certainty we can actually achieve. Intelligent mastery of a risky world can only be achieved through practice.

Heidegger, too, drew surreptitiously on pragmatist insights in his analyses of "equipment" [*Zeug*], "readiness-to-hand" [*Zuhandenheit*], and "context of involvement" [*Bewandtniszusammenhang*] in *Being and Time*.[2] Heidegger's concept of "being-in-the-world" also shares the anti-Platonist thrust of pragmatism. On the other hand, in this way he seeks to disclose the ontological dimension of the authentic beyond the realm of everyday life, which is devalued as "ontic." In the later Heidegger, the Platonic Ideas are drawn into the current of events in the history of being. But the ontological difference has the effect of preserving the *chorismos* (i.e. separation or division) between the extraordinary and the everyday, which Dewey levels out. Heidegger associates the attitude of submissive "remembrance" [*Andenken*] of the fate [*Geschicke*] of a higher power with the privileged access to truth which he reserves for poets and thinkers. By contrast, Dewey begins his investigations with a forking of paths along which "[m]an who lives in a world of hazards is compelled to seek for security." With the path of "supplication," which is reminiscent of Heidegger's fatalistic reflection on being, he contrasts the activity of inventors: "The other course is to invent arts and by their means turn the powers of nature to account."[3]

Finally, this confidence in the civilizing power of mastery of nature also separates Dewey from those with whom he shares the critique of the separation of theory from practice, though certainly not the critique of "instrumental reason." Understood in an operational sense, the natural sciences are inherently oriented to the acquisition of technically applicable knowledge. Technical success makes them, for Dewey, an unimpeachable model for problem-solving behavior in general. Of course, Dewey expects too much from the application of the experimental attitude to all practical questions when he assumes that moral and political value judgments can also be justified by appeal to the conditions of the success of an instrumental practice of realizing values. In moral questions, the insights of his friend George Herbert Mead into the role of perspective-taking in social interactions could have led him further.

Nevertheless, Dewey uncovered the cognitive roots of a lifeworld practice designed for coping with the contingencies and failures involved in interactions with a disconcerting reality. The quest for certainty is the obverse side of a consciousness of risk which is aware of the fact that enduring "adaptive" behavioral patterns can develop only through productive coping with disappointments and the progressive mastering of problems. What sets human beings apart as active beings is precisely this problem-solving behavior: knowing how to analyze a problematic situation and knowing that there is no other authority to fall back on than one's own intelligent efforts.

Dewey is at any rate immune to a tragic heightening or existentialist elevation of this *situation humaine*. He refuses to play off depth against surface, risk against normality, the event of being [*Ereignis*] against the habitual, the mystical against the trivial. Dewey incites, rather than excites. As a democratic thinker, he is egalitarian through and through. This is why his reception in the Federal Republic – the "old" Federal Republic, as we say nowadays – could only begin when the young conservative attitude toward an exalted past had begun to dissolve. He would also be a better patron for the Berlin Republic.

10

Richard Rorty, *Achieving Our Country*

Richard Rorty is much more than just a renowned philosopher. He is also a philosophical author with literary ambitions who effortlessly masters a variety of literary genres, including the essay, the public address, and the polemic, in addition to the academic treatise and the expert interpretation. With *Achieving our Country*, Rorty extends his repertoire to include something akin to the patriotic manifesto. The book will shortly appear in a German translation under the title *Stolz auf unser Land* ("Proud of our Country").[1] The intended audience of Rorty's invocation of American civil religion are the educated among the scoffers. The book is an indictment of the "cultural Left" which has become infected with Heidegger's cultural pessimism and plays the role of the opinionated hand-wringer who comments from the sidelines on a world in disarray.

Four different stories are interwoven in this secularized revivalist sermon: the political biography of its author, the history of the polarization between the old and the new Left, the lament over the depoliticization of the most recent, academically domesticated Left, and, finally, a paean to the grand tradition stretching from Emerson through Walt Whitman to Dewey, which formed the intellectual backbone of all American progressive movements.

Rorty's political biography is shaped as much by the anti-communism of the 1950s as by the opposition to the Vietnam War. He sees the Cold War as the legitimate continuation of the war against fascism. These autobiographical remarks are scattered throughout a history of the American Left which culminates in 1964 in a tragic split with the "new Left." In hindsight, the anti-communist activism of former Trotskyites during the postwar era blends with the older reformism of the early twentieth century and the New Deal of the Roosevelt era into a single "social democratic" movement. During the 1960s, this duly collided with a protest movement that turned against "the system" as such. Radical students drew sufficient strength for a successful mobilization against the calamitous Vietnam War from their pseudo-revolutionary self-understanding, but at the cost of the demise of the reformist Left.

The history of the cultural Left begins with this ambivalent judgment. During the 1970s, the henceforth theoretically sublimated spirit of revolt migrated from social science departments to literature departments, with the deconstruction of philosophical texts replacing the critique of political economy. A heightened sensitivity to linguistic forms of discrimination supplanted moral outrage over structurally anchored social inequalities. Rorty's polemic against "the politics of difference," nourished by the spirit of deconstruction, is not without a certain piquancy. For it was Rorty himself, more than any other figure, who was instrumental in lifting the ban on the works of Heidegger, Foucault, and Derrida, whose intellectual influence he now condemns, in controversies with the orthodox bastions of analytical philosophy. Today he somberly observes that the cultural Left has bred a "school of resentment" in which students lose touch with their indignation over social injustice, while simultaneously forfeiting the measure of confidence they would need to throw themselves into the real work of politics.

Rorty's criticism is spurred by a sympathy born of pent-up anger over growing poverty, oppression, and intolerance in his own country. He laments the defeatism of those who turn their backs on traditional leftist causes and dissipate their energies in derivative intellectual controversies. His manifesto calls for a return to the authentic, the only specifically American, tradition of political pragmatism. Although this tradition took its inspiration from Europe, and in particular from German idealism, the naturalistic appropriation of Hegel in Whitman's hymns and Dewey's writings brought forth a distinctively American form of Young Hegelianism, energized by the modern spirit of democracy, science, and technology. This tradition found an audible echo in Germany only after World War II, and lent impetus to the pro-American segment of the German Left.

This provides the background for the rhetorically brilliant chapter on Whitman and Dewey, which begins with the words: "National pride is to countries what self-respect is to individuals: a necessary condition for self-development." As news of this Stanford lecture first made its way across the Atlantic, some saw in it grounds for triumphalism mingled with *Schadenfreude*. There was talk of the famous philosopher's political "turn." Wasn't he reading the riot act to his political friends? Wasn't he giving his rootless colleagues – all of them bloodless constitutional patriots – the necessary remedial instruction in the subject "self-confident nation"?

But Rorty rejects these overtures from the Right. After all, our neo-conservatives have always appealed to the nation, even though from essentially functionalist motives. In the neo-conservative world-view, healthy national consciousness figures alongside religion and the family as a traditional bulwark that provides free compensation for the social hardships produced by freewheeling economic deregulation. Today the Schäubles and the Stoibers draw from this reservoir of ideas when they use the issue of dual citizenship (tomorrow it will no doubt be same-sex marriage) as a pretext for stirring up the murky xenophobic sentiments of the duller sections of the population with nationalistic slogans.[2] But these right-wing populists will find no comfort in Rorty's manifesto. Rorty's patriotism is of an early romantic pedigree, not the traditionalistic form of patriotism of the romantics who became pious in their old age.

The nation, for Rorty, is not a quasi-natural substrate that functions as a shock-absorber cushioning the population from the undesirable consequences of modernization. For him, the nation signifies the self-creation of a deliberating civil society – a work in progress, not a gift of nature. National identities only take shape in the current of public discourses. They are a matter of "what we should try to make of ourselves." Such discourses are not free of emotion. On the contrary, the history and the current politics of one's country awaken "feelings of intense shame and glowing pride." It seems as though the citizens can hardly achieve a reasonable ethical and political self-understanding "unless pride outweighs shame."

Already the opening pages of Rorty's book contain statements that sound suspicious. They seem to lend grist to the mill of those who have no need of neo-conservatism to feed their yearning for the recovery of "normality." Recently, even respected members of the political and social elite have been making a public display of their inability to distinguish between what belongs in the Paulskirche and what on the analyst's couch. On live television, they accord a writer who no longer wants to be reminded of "our shame" a standing ovation. Even the eminent left-liberal publisher is so overwhelmed by the resurgent feelings of his youth that he can only bemoan the planned memorial for the murdered European Jews: "Now, in the center of the recently recovered capital of Berlin, a monument is supposed to be erected to remind us of our enduring shame."[3]

However, even members of this generation won't find any encouragement in Rorty, who recommends that they perform an interesting thought-experiment. What makes us moral beings? The fact that there are actions that are such that we know that we should die rather than do such a thing. Now imagine that you had done something like that, and yet were still alive. Someone in that position would have to choose between, on the one hand, committing suicide or living a life devoid of self-respect and, on the other, attempting to go on living in a way that lends credibility to the resolution "never to do such a thing again." Rorty recommends the latter alternative even in the case of political crimes for which the members of a nation are in a sense collectively liable. No crime that "a nation has done should make it impossible for a constitutional democracy to regain self-respect." Here Rorty is thinking primarily of his own country. But he also has in mind another country which he knows particularly well: the "old" Federal Republic of Germany, whose citizens have learned over the decades that their future depends on taking a conscious stand on the criminal past of their own community.

Rorty advocates a strictly secular conception of politics. He opposes a political-theological self-understanding that crystallizes around the concept of sin. He emboldens his readers to become politically self-aware, to embrace a forward-looking form of activism that has emancipated itself from the tyranny which a repressed past exercises over the future. The optimistic tone of this frank and unpretentious pragmatism, at least, may seem to be in harmony with the most recent mindset of the current German ruling generation. Isn't it finally about time to insist a bit more boldly on the normality of this land of the later-born?

In 1995, as the controversy with the New Right over the interpretation of May 8, 1945 had just concluded, a book title like *The Normality of a Berlin Republic* still had an unambiguous meaning.[4] It clearly invoked the "dialectic of normalization," the fact that here in Germany the emergence of halfway normal social conditions after the breakdown in civilization was made possible only by eschewing a false sense of normality. But since the change in government last year, the expressions "normality" and "Berlin republic" have undergone a Left-national redefinition; their meaning has been reversed and now signifies a "fitness for the future" unburdened of ritual commemoration. The contribution of the Chancellor's Office, which is as sensitive to the media as it is normatively hollow, to enriching an increasingly bleak intellectual landscape is studied silence on the division of the nation into German Germans and Jewish Germans and proposals for a more visitor-friendly design for the Berlin Holocaust memorial. And all the while the Chancellor, with his catchy nationalist slogans, is robbing the nonplussed leader writers of the *Frankfurter Allgemeine Zeitung* of their favorite conservative catchphrases.

But even the normalizers of the more harmless variety should not expect any philosophical support from an author who has chosen the title of his book with care. Rorty borrowed the challenge to make something of our country, to "achieve our country," from a novel that cannot be accused of turning its back on the darkest chapter of American history. In it, James Baldwin reminds his white fellow citizens unremittingly of the oppression and exploitation of Native Americans, Blacks, and Mexicans. Yet he never gives up the hope of fighting together for a better America in the future based on keeping alive the memory of a divided past.

This "pride in one's country" is a very American pride. As is only to be expected from a manifesto like this, its statements only take on a precise meaning in contexts that are not ours. Rorty himself reminds us of this fact in a footnote on the German discussion of "constitutional patriotism." None of the stories Rorty relates can be translated directly. The political biography of a "red diaper baby" born in New York in 1931 is not even typical for most American intellectuals of his generation. The history of the American Left is nourished by different traditions and confronts different social contexts and historical events from those of the Left in Europe. There is likewise no European counterpart of a pragmatism that equates love of country with passion for industrial progress, social justice, and democracy. Even the cultural Left which has reigned in the United States for the past two decades does not have a counterpart in German or French universities. Nevertheless, the German Left, which has also succumbed to defeatism, could use some encouragement. They will impress nobody with their clever studies of the nation-state, the future of Europe, and globalization as long as they remain cloistered in the academic ghetto.

Rorty exhorts "his" Left to fight for a better America. This marks a return to the intellectual roots of the political culture of a country that coalesced into a nation-state only in the twentieth century. Starting from completely different initial conditions, European states still face the task of forming a closer union. If Rorty's patriotic manifesto has any message for us Europeans, then it is the call to engage in public debates over the political self-understanding of European citizens who must construct a pan-European democracy if they want to defuse the social time-bombs of an admittedly highly productive single market and currency through common policies.

11

Robert Brandom, *Making it Explicit*

Six years ago, Richard Rorty called my attention to a book by one of his students: "This actually carries out the formal pragmatics that you need." That was the first time I had heard the name of its author, whose book has just appeared in German translation under the title *Expressive Vernunft* ("Expressive Reason").[1] Suhrkamp Verlag can take the credit for making accessible to the German public a 1,000-page text whose philosophical importance is proportionate to its scope. The pathos of working a complex idea of great speculative power through to its conclusion is reminiscent of the intellectual discipline of Edmund Husserl. In an era of frenzied stagnation, when confessional prose, dismissive polemics, fake profundity, and science-fiction science threaten to drown out everything else, a work that is driven solely by the substance of its own inquiry comes as a breath of fresh air. It looms large above an intellectual landscape in which the poverty of issues and ideas is disguised by empty talk of "generations" and "lifestyles."

Robert Brandom, a colleague of John McDowell's at the University of Pittsburgh philosophy department, has employed all the resources of logic and semantics to recover the concept of objective spirit [*objektiver Geist*], which has until now remained alien to analytic philosophy, in the form of a theory of discourse. He analyzes everyday communication into the moves in a game of argumentation in which each player carefully registers what the other participants accomplish with their speech acts: namely, the commitments and entitlements that they thereby incur. Reason unfolds in the form of a shared communicative practice.

Brandom confidently addresses the problems generated by the tradition extending from Frege to Dummett from within, as it were. By the same token, however, with his idiosyncratic terminology he also wants to create a language in which subjects capable of speech and action can first understand themselves as subjects of mental states and normative commitments. Although this esoteric pragmatics of speech is intended for fellow specialists, the author's idealist ambitions clearly extend beyond the academy. Brandom understands his theory in good Hegelian fashion as a contemporary attempt of the human mind [*Geist*] to achieve self-awareness as it unfolds in the practices of a communication community. Brandom explores the practice of linguistic communication, which is constitutive for us as logical beings who operate with concepts. He seeks to clarify the normative self-understanding of subjects for whom "reasons count." Even the pragmatist's desublimated "kingdom of ends" is a universe of rational beings who submit themselves to the non-coercive authority of good reasons. Such beings demand mutual accountability for their utterances and make their interactions dependent on the discursive practice of reciprocal accountability.

A large-scale undertaking like this has a hard time of it in the United States, where the leading philosophers build their careers on carefully written articles rather than on thick books. In addition, Brandom's speculative impulse clashes with a naturalistic *zeitgeist* that harmonizes with the scientistic self-understanding of the American scientific establishment. In Germany, conditions are more favorable for the reception of the book, a process which is already well under way. Like Brandom, in this country we tend to see the shadow of Frege behind Wittgenstein and the shadow of Kant behind Frege. Even Reichenbach and Carnap still drew on Kant, whereas the school of Quine and Davidson remains loyal to their Humean roots even when it does not strip the mental of all normativity from the beginning. Here Brandom meets with an interest in the pragmatics of speech which draws on indigenous sources, specifically, philosophical hermeneutics, the constructivism of the Erlangen school, and a Kantian assimilation of Peircean semiotics and speech act theory.

Furthermore, Brandom's reception is facilitated by the fact that his book comes in the wake of the classics of American pragmatism to which all doors now stand open. Pragmatism, which is the only authentically American philosophy, is deeply shaped by the spirit of Hegelian philosophy, interpreted in intersubjectivistic and natu-

ralistic terms. In spite of this intellectual affinity, the pragmatist tradition put down roots in Germany only after World War II. In contrast to Marx and Kierkegaard, the American branch of Young
Hegelianism possesses a vital concept of democracy – a conception
of civil society which understands itself as an experimenting and
learning communication community. Pragmatism formed a bridge
between German and American philosophy from the very beginning.
But now the transatlantic flow of ideas has reversed direction.
Whereas Peirce, James, Mead, and Dewey still looked to Germany,
today it is we who are learning from their American students.

In my view, Brandom's innovative accomplishment consists in a
seamless combination of Wilfrid Sellars' inferential semantics with
the pragmatics of a communicative practice oriented to validity
claims. On this approach, the lexicon of language resolves itself into
a network of material implications. The conceptual content of communicative expressions is articulated in the fact that a speaker is
legitimated in the eyes of an interpreter in making certain moves in
the game of argumentation. Everyone interprets everyone else. Each
keeps tabs on the argumentative rights and obligations to which
others commit themselves with their validity claims, whether they
are aware of it or not. The whole burden of constructing and evaluating valid utterances thereby falls on the shoulders of the participants in discourse themselves. For Brandom investigates how the
participants manage to localize a speech act within the network of
obligations and entitlements to which speakers commit themselves
with the corresponding utterances.

Brandom holds his readers in suspense over nine difficult chapters
with a single question: how can participants in discourse break out
of their self-enclosed practice of reciprocal attribution and assessment of validity claims and bring their language into relation to an
independently existing world, which must ultimately vouch for the
objectivity of their judgments? The distinction between language and
world must always be made within language itself. Brandom's subtle
and entirely unconventional explanation for this amounts to the
claim that this difference between propositions and facts – ultimately,
between what we take to be true and what is true – can be traced
back to a difference between the social perspectives of speaker and
interpreter. After all, an interpreter doesn't have to accept a truth
claim that he ascribes to someone else, for example, when he con-
siders the problematic presuppositions or implication to which a

speaker implicitly commits himself with his utterance without fully realizing it.

On this account, the objective conceptual content of the expressions employed serves as a critical standard. But who vouches for the objectivity of concepts we draw from our vocabulary? If I use the concept "copper" incorrectly, then an expert in chemistry can certainly explain to me why I could not have made a particular utterance if I had properly understood the precise meaning of the term. But in that case, we must follow Hilary Putnam in asking what is the nature of the authority on which this scientific judgment is based. It seems that we can learn things from our practical dealings with nature – things which we cannot learn from discursive dealings with one another. In the course of an informative interview (in the *Deutsche Zeitschrift für Philosophie*, 6/1999), Brandom gives an evasive response to a clever student who posed this question. His book did not deal with the problem of concept-*formation*, he claimed, only with the *use* of available concepts in discourse.

The transition to objective idealism represents a possible way of closing this gap while remaining within the perspective of participants in conversation. It is not yet clear whether Brandom really makes this transition. The book's German title, *Expressive Vernunft*, is meant to suggest that he does. For "expressive reason" has the connotation of the self-unfolding of a mind [*Geist*] that by its very nature connects an intrinsically propositionally structured world with our discursive practices [*discursive Geist*]. The original English title is *Making it Explicit*, which alludes to the method of spelling out the intuitive knowledge of competent speakers from the participant perspective.. This procedure initially has the trivial sense of translating *know-how* into *knowing that*, something we do unavoidably when we rationally reconstruct skills. But Brandom lends this method an emphatic meaning. He wants to reconstruct a process by which the mind progressively raises itself to ever-higher levels via the stages of the self-referential vocabulary of higher-level logical and semantic concepts. His aim is to solve after his own fashion the task which Hegel set himself in his *Logic*: on Brandom's reading, absolute knowledge for Hegel is the stage at which we have completely developed our logical resources.

Brandom shares with his American colleagues Robert Pippin and Terry Pinkard a deflationary understanding of Hegel's "absolute knowledge." We eagerly await whether Brandom will remain firmly planted on pragmatist ground in his next book on Hegel, or whether he will allow his metaphysical impulse to take wing. Brandom reminds us in one place of his teacher Rorty's claim that the work of Wilfrid Sellars tied down Hegel's spirit in Carnap's chains. Brandom himself flirts with the idea of leading Rorty's spirit by the leash along the path from Wittgenstein via Kant to Hegel. I regard this as a viable alternative to the prevailing symbiosis of the late Wittgenstein and the late Heidegger.

Part VII

Jerusalem, Athens, and Rome

I conducted the following conversation with Eduardo Mendieta, who is strongly influenced by South American liberation theology and who currently teaches philosophy at New York State University at Stony Brook (summer of 1999). It originally appeared in the *Jahrbuch für Politische Theologie* 3 (1999): 190–211.

12

A Conversation about God and the World

Question: The slogan of the day is "globalization," even though nobody knows exactly what it means. Some view it as a new political, economic, technological, social, or even ecological, regime. Others contest the qualitative difference between this break and other epochal markers like modernity, postmodernity, and postcoloniality. They see globalization as modernity become self-reflexive. Curiously, the question of religion remains present, but unarticulated, in these reflections. To what extent do you see religion as a precursor, a catalyst, or a condition of possibility of modernity and globalization?

J. H.: The themes of the Judeo-Christian heritage help to explain the cultural, though not the social, modernization of the West. Through the reception of Greek philosophy (if one thinks of Toledo, for example), these impulses were also combined with the impetus of Islam. We should also remember that for all three monotheistic religions it was primarily the heretical movements and schisms which preserved a sensitivity for the more radical forms of revelation. From a sociological point of view, the modern forms of consciousness encompassing abstract law, modern science, and autonomous art (with the secularization and independence of easel art at its core) could never have developed apart from the organizational forms of Hellenized Christianity and the Roman Church, without the universities, monasteries, and cathedrals. This is especially true for the development of mentalities.

In contrast with archaic mythic narratives, the idea of God – the idea of the single, invisible God the Creator and Redeemer – already signified a breakthrough to an entirely new perspective. With this idea, the finite human mind [*endlicher Geist*] achieved a standpoint that transcends everything this-worldly. But only with the transition to modernity does the knowing and morally judging subject assimilate the divine standpoint in such a way that it accomplishes two momentous idealizations. On the one hand, it objectifies external nature as the totality of states of affairs and events which are connected in a law-like manner and, on the other, it expands the familiar social world into an unbounded community of all responsible agents. In this way, the door is opened for reason to penetrate the opaque world in both dimensions, in the form of the cognitive rationalization of a fully objectified nature and of the social-cognitive rationalization of the totality of morally regulated interpersonal relations.

My impression is that Buddhism is the only other world religion which achieved a comparable level of abstraction and which, structurally regarded, carried out a similar conceptualization of the divine standpoint. Unlike the monotheistic worldviews, Eastern religions are based not on the acting person but on the impersonal consciousness of an indeterminate "something." They push the dynamic of abstraction in the opposite direction, not through the heightening of personal capacities in the direction of the "omnipotent," "omniscient," and "all-loving" God, but through the ever more thorough negation of all conceivable properties of an object of perception and judgment. In this way, Buddhism approaches the vanishing point of a pure or radical "nothing," or what remains once we have abstracted from everything that makes an arbitrary something into a particular entity – the not-something which also found expression in Malevich's black square. The same cognitive operation which led the Greeks to the "being of beings," following a theoretical impulse, here leads, driven by a moral impulse, to a "nothing" that has sloughed off everything constitutive of a thing in the world.

As it happens, however, cultural and social modernization did not begin in the regions dominated by Buddhism. For, in the West, Christianity not only fulfilled the initial cognitive conditions for modern structures of consciousness; it also fostered a range of motivations that formed the major theme of the economic and ethical research of Max Weber. Christianity has functioned for the normative self-understanding of modernity as more than a mere precursor or a catalyst. Egalitarian universalism, from which sprang the ideas of freedom and social solidarity, of an autonomous conduct of life and emancipation, of the individual morality of conscience, human rights, and democracy, is the direct heir to the Judaic ethic of justice and the Christian ethic of love. This legacy, substantially unchanged, has been the object of continual critical appropriation and reinterpretation. To this day, there is no alternative to it. And in light of the current challenges of a postnational constellation, we continue to draw on the substance of this heritage. Everything else is just idle postmodern talk.

To be sure, the globalization of markets, that is, the electronic networking of financial markets and the accelerated mobility of capital, have led to a transnational economic regime that has markedly diminished the leading industrialized nations' scope for action. But the intensification and expansion of communication and commerce only creates a new infrastructure, not a new orientation or a new form of consciousness. This new stage in the development of capitalism takes place within the essentially unchanging horizon of social modernity and the associated normative self-understanding which developed after the end of the eighteenth century. As I said, religion and the Church served as important pacemakers for this mentality; but the same cannot be said for the emergence of globalized commerce and communication. Rather, Christianity is as much affected and challenged by the unforeseen consequences of this new infrastructure as are other forms of "objective Spirit."

Question: That's just what I wanted to ask. The relationship between modernity and globalization, on the one hand, and religion, on the other, also comes into play in such a way that contemporary forms of religious consciousness and, one must add, of theology are themselves the offspring of modernity and globalization. To what extent can contemporary forms of religion be understood as products of modernity and globalization, both with regard to institutions and practices of faith and to beliefs and forms of experience?

J. H.: The Christian churches must meet the challenges of globalization by drawing more deeply on their own normative resources. Ecumenism is only now becoming ecumenical in a non-paternalistic sense; only now is the Church becoming a polycentric world Church, a topic that has engaged my friend Johannes Baptist Metz. The universalism of the world religions is only now acquiring a strongly intercultural meaning; the Christian ethic is only now extending itself into a truly inclusive global ethos, a project which Hans Küng has advocated. But your question aims deeper than this. If I am correct, it refers to the transformation of religious consciousness which began in the West with the Reformation and which since then has also spread to other world religions – in other words, the "modernization" of faith. This same process of modernization for which religion and the Church fulfilled important initial conditions brought forth a secularized society and a pluralism of worldviews which then, in turn, necessitated a cognitive restructuring of religious faith and Church practice.

Revealed religions are transmitted in the dogmatic form of a "doctrine." But in the West, Christian doctrine developed into a scientific [*wissenschaftlich*] theology through the conceptual medium and scholastic forms of philosophy. In modern societies, religious teachings must accustom themselves to the unavoidable competition with other forms of faith and claims to truth. They no longer move in a self-contained universe governed, so to speak, by their own absolute truth. Every religious teaching today encounters the pluralism of different forms of religious truth, as well as the skepticism of secular scientific knowledge which owes its social authority to its declared fallibility and a learning process based on unceasing revision. Religious dogmatics and the consciousness of believers must harmonize the illocutionary meaning of religious speech, the affirmation of the truth of a religious statement, with both facts. Each religious confession must adopt a relationship with the competing messages of other religions no less than with the objections of science and a secularized, semi-learned common sense.

Thus, modern faith becomes reflexive. For it can only stabilize itself through self-critical awareness of the status it assumes within a universe of discourse restricted by secular knowledge and shared with other religions. This decentered background consciousness of the relativity of one's own position, which, to be sure, must not lead to the relativization of articles of faith themselves, is characteristic of the modern form of religious faith. Furthermore, the reflexive consciousness which has learnt to see itself through the eyes of others is constitutive of what John Rawls calls the reasonableness of "reasonable comprehensive doctrines." This has the important political consequence that the community of the faithful can know why it must refrain from the use of violence, and especially of state-sponsored violence, as a means of imposing religious truths. In this sense, what we call the "modernization of faith" is an important cognitive presupposition for the realization of religious toleration and the construction of a neutral state power.

We describe as "fundamentalist" those religious movements which, given the cognitive constraints of modern life, nevertheless persist in propagating, and even practicing, a return to the exclusivity of premodern religious outlooks. Fundamentalism lacks the epistemic innocence of those old empires, which could still be experienced as somehow limitless, in which the world religions first flourished. Only contemporary China provides a glimmer of this sense of imperial boundlessness, which originally grounded the limited "universalism" of the world religions. But modern conditions are compatible only with a strict, if you will, Kantian form of universalism. This is why fundamentalism is the wrong answer to an epistemological situation which imposes insight into the inevitability of religious toleration, and thereby enjoins on the faithful the burden of enduring the secularization of knowledge and the pluralism of images of the world, regardless of their own religious truths.

Question: Religion is also a form of human communication and, as such, is not unaffected by transformations in the means of communication. Today, telecommunications are revolutionizing all means and modes of communication. Are we witnessing the obsolescence of older forms of human interaction and are the new communications media bringing forth new religions, new churches, new forms of piety and prayer?

J. H.: I can't say much on this point, since this is the kind of question that can only be answered "from within," from the viewpoint of participants. And, sociologically speaking, I have not studied any of the new, de-institutionalized and de-differentiated forms of religiosity. All the great world religions experienced anti-clerical revival movements critical of existing institutions, mystical movements, even subjectivistic forms of devotional enthusiasm, a case in point being German pietism. This same impulse survives today in different forms. But what I nowadays observe from a distance in the "esoterica" sections of bookshops strikes me more as a symptom of ego weakness and regression, an expression of a yearning for an impossible return to mythical forms of thought, magical practices, and closed worldviews which the Church transcended with its battle against "heathenism." But history teaches us that religious sects can be sources of innovation. So maybe not everything on the market is Californian claptrap or neopaganism.

But somehow discursive debate seems to be lacking in this area – perhaps even the possibility of a serious discourse. Reading Aquinas' *Summa Contra Gentiles*, I am struck by the complexity, the level of differentiation, the gravity, and the rigor of the dialectical argument. I am an admirer of Aquinas. He represents a form of intellect that could vouch for its own authenticity. That such a tower of strength among the shifting sands of religiosity is nowhere to be found today is simply a fact. In a homogenizing media society, everything loses its seriousness – perhaps even institutionalized Christianity itself.

Question: In your work you sometimes speak of Europe's mission to the world, of the prospect of a "second chance" in history for a united Europe. But is this prospect not compromised precisely by Europe's relationship to Christianity? For example, if one reads between the lines of most of the philosophers of the global state, like Fukuyama or Huntington, one finds that they understand globalization as the continuation of the Christian civilizing project, and whatever stands in its way is dismissed as "oriental" despotism or Muslim fundamentalism, etc. From this evangelical point of view, globalization is, as it were, inoculated against the threat of "infection" from non-Western cultures.

J. H.: Well, we won't argue over the "unholy trinity" of colonialism, Christianity, and Eurocentrism. The dark side of the mirror of modernization, which would like to present exclusively the image of the spread of civilization, human rights, and democracy, has already been more or less explored. But, in the end, egalitarian universalism, which today's neoliberal apologists for a politically unregulated global economic regime trumpet just as loudly as yesterday's colonial masters did Christianity, also offers the only convincing criteria for criticizing the miserable state of our economically fragmented, stratified, and unpacified world society. Who would still want to justify the monstrously brutal process of global modernization from the fifteenth century onwards from a normative point of view? Yet, the current state of the world, "the modern condition," to which there is no obvious alternative, is after all not something for which we in the present have to assume responsibility or which we must justify retrospectively.

As the Pol Pot regime in Cambodia, the "shining Path" in Peru, and the impoverished dictatorship in North Korea illustrate, there is no longer any reasonable exit-option from a capitalist world society after the failed experiment of Soviet communism. Transformations of global capitalism that point beyond a permanent state of self-propelling "creative destruction" now seem possible only from within. This is why we need a form of self-referential politics directed toward strengthening capacities for political action themselves and toward reining in an uncontrolled economic dynamic both within and, above all, beyond the currently still authoritative level of nation-state actors. I have described this in my book *The Postnational Constellation*.[1] The fact that we can only operate under conditions of social modernity not of our own choosing obviously does not imply that we must act as missionaries of a Western culture that brought all this forth.

Let's take the example of human rights. Notwithstanding their European origins, human rights today represent the universal language in which global relations can be normatively regulated. In Asia, Africa, and South America, they constitute the sole language in which the opponents and victims of murderous regimes and civil wars can raise their voices against violence, repression, and persecution, and against violations of their human dignity. But as human rights have won acceptance as a transcultural language, disagreements between cultures over their proper interpretation have also intensified. Insofar as this intercultural discourse on human rights is conducted in a spirit of reciprocal recognition, it can also lead the West to a decentered understanding of a normative construction that is no longer the property of Europeans and may no longer exclusively reflect the particularities of this one culture.

To be sure, the West still retains privileged access to the resources of power, wealth, and knowledge in our world. But it is in our own best interest that the Western project of developing a just and peaceful global civilization should not be discredited from the outset. Thus the Judeo-Hellenic-Christian West must reflect on one of its greatest cultural achievements, the capacity for decentering one's own perspectives, for self-reflection, and for self-critical distancing from one's own traditions. The West must refrain from using any non-discursive means in the hermeneutical conversation between cultures and must

become just one voice among others. In a word, overcoming Eurocentrism demands that the West make proper use of its own cognitive resources. This is, God knows, easier said than done, as the
current example of the selective prosecutions and the problems of
implementing human rights policy in the former Yugoslavia illustrate.
But that is a different topic.

Question: Let me pose the question more pointedly. Can we talk of
the West without mentioning Athens, Rome, and Jerusalem in the
same breath? And, conversely, can we speak of a postnational global
order without thinking of the long history of religious conflicts and
the ever-present possibility of their intensification?

J. H.: You correctly point to the internal tensions along the fault lines
of Western culture. Jerusalem, Athens, and Rome – this is the characteristic tension between monotheism, science [*Wissenschaft*], and
the republican tradition which the West has always had to endure,
without assimilating one to the other. As regards the relation between
Athens and Jerusalem, the Hellenization of Christianity, that is, the
theological rationalization of the redemptive message, involved an
inherent tendency to water down the essence of Christianity. Job's
question, the question of God's justice in the face of the existential
experience of suffering and of annihilation in godforsaken darkness,
loses its radicality within the horizon of Greek thought, and even
in the Church fathers. Where was God in Auschwitz? Along the
Rome–Jerusalem axis, we can observe a similar slackening of tension:
on the one hand, the secularization and politicization of the biblical
message and, on the other, the political-theological hollowing-out of
the rational core of a secularized politics. Finally, we Germans are
also familiar with the cultural-religious nimbus of the pretentious but
depoliticized neo-humanism which sublimates Roman republicanism
into Greek intellectualism, so that the pragmatism of daily life is
submerged in the dizzying aura of the extraordinary. Among the
Germans, Brecht – not Hannah Arendt – belongs among the few
party faithful of "Rome" who recognized the fatal consequences of
German classicism's fixation on Greek antiquity.
    These symbiotic aberrations occur when the opposed elements of
a tension-laden cultural synthesis lose their distinctive character. This
can also be seen in the relation between philosophy and religion,
for the existential meaning of the liberation of the individual soul

through the salvation promised by God the Redeemer cannot be assimilated to the contemplative elevation and the intuitive fusion of the human mind with the absolute. Things are much the same at the global level with the tension among the various cultures and world religions. Particular cultures can only make a positive contribution to the emerging world culture if their distinctive character is respected. This tension must be stabilized, though not resolved, if the threads of intercultural discourse are not to be broken.

Question: If we examine the philosophical achievements, ruptures, and continuities of the West, we see a perennial confrontation, but also the connection, with the Judeo-Christian tradition. This confrontation with and claim to the legacy of Athens and Rome and, albeit painfully and reluctantly, of Jerusalem, is especially marked in German philosophy from Jakob Böhme and Meister Eckhart, through Martin Luther, Kant, Hegel, and Marx to Heidegger, Löwith, Bloch, Adorno, Horkheimer, and, of course, Benjamin. One could almost say that Christendom survived in the halls of German philosophy. If this is the case, how can European philosophy open itself up to the cultures of the world without reflecting anew on its own religious core?

J. H.: Yes, I see intense encounters with "strong" traditions of other cultures as an opportunity to become more fully aware of our own roots, hence also of our rootedness in the Judeo-Christian tradition. As long as participants inhabit the same discursive universe, there is no hermeneutic impulse to reflect on self-evident background motives which remain unspoken. This spur to reflection does not prevent intercultural understanding, but rather first makes it possible. All participants must become aware of the particularity of their respective intellectual presuppositions before the shared discursive presuppositions, interpretations, and value orientations can come to light.

Today the West confronts other cultures in the shape of the overwhelming scientific and technological infrastructure of a capitalist world civilization. This civilization is the materialization of our forms of rationality. By contrast, other cultures do not initially confront us as alien societies, since their structures remind us of previous phases of our own social development. What does strike us as alien in other cultures is primarily the distinctive character of the religions at their core. We see their religion as the source of inspiration of the other culture. This explains not only the continuing relevance of Max Weber, but also the challenge to European philosophy to pose precisely the question that you are insisting on here.

However, I would draw sharper distinctions among the principal figures within the German tradition whom you have named. In comparison with English, French, or American philosophy, Germany has had relatively few politically minded intellectuals. The Roman-republican heritage only comes into its own with Kant and Reinhold, Heine and Marx. On the other hand, the experience of the French Revolution inspired the Tübingen seminarians, Hegel, Schelling, and Hölderlin, to reconcile Athens with Jerusalem, and both of them with a modernity that derives its essential normative self-understanding from the egalitarian, universalistic spirit of the Jewish and Christian traditions. In this context, Hegel's main concern was to subject basic metaphysical concepts to a dynamic dialectical reinterpretation within the medium of soteriological [*heilsgeschichtlich*] thought. Nevertheless, one can distinguish within German philosophy to the present day between a more aesthetic-Platonist line and one oriented to social philosophy and the philosophy of history.

The tradition that remains dedicated to the ontological and cosmological concerns of the Greek tradition persists not only in the form of classical philosophical idealism, as in Dieter Henrich's theory of self-consciousness. The metaphysical interest in the constitution of being as such also persists in the language of formal semantics and epistemology. It can even be dealt with in the language of naturalism, for example, in the current discussion of the relation between mind and body. This philosophical mainstream differs in its basic concerns and basic concepts from the philosophical schools which were revolutionized by historical thought. The latter adopted the existential or world-historical themes which were previously the preserve of theology and its soteriological reflections. The exemplary figures here were, of course, the great outsiders of the nineteenth century, Marx, Kierkegaard, and Nietzsche. Here also belong all the movements which offered a diagnosis of their times and promoted categories of lived historical experience into basic philosophical concepts. I have in mind concepts like sociality, language, praxis, embodiment, contingency, space of action, historical time, intersubjective understanding, individuality, freedom, emancipation, domination, the anticipation of one's own death, and so on.

However, I would again emphasize the tradition of dialectical thinking within these historically minded and epoch-sensitive currents which were more deeply influenced by "Jerusalem" than by "Athens," by the religious rather than the Greek metaphysical heritage. This line, extending from Jakob Böhme through Oetinger and Schelling, Hegel, and Marx to Bloch, Benjamin, and, if you like, Foucault, stands opposed to another, mystical line of thought that begins with Meister Eckhart and ends for the present with Heidegger and perhaps Wittgenstein. Whereas mystical contemplation is speechless, privileging a mode of intuition or recollection that repudiates the rational orientation of discursive thought, dialectical thought has always criticized the notions of intellectual intuition and intuitive access to the supposedly immediate. In the productive force of negation, dialectics recognizes its own proper impetus, the motor of a self-critical reason which Hegel celebrated as the rose in the cross of the present. In this tradition, philosophy takes seriously the *theologoumenon* of the divine become flesh, the unconditioned character of moral obligation in the face of radical evil, the finitude of human freedom, the fallibility of spirit, and individual mortality. Dialectics addresses the problem of theodicy, the struggle with the negativity of an inverted world. Such a world could never be experienced as something negative, as something "inverted," if it retained the naturalistic character of an indifferent, merely contingent, occurrence, so to speak. For example, in my student years I was already interested in Schelling's *On the Essence of Human Freedom.*

Question: Many people, including yourself, have remarked that the Frankfurt School would not have been possible without Marx, but not without Judaism either. Most members of the first generation of the Frankfurt School were Jews. They developed their critique of society and, in light of this critique, their view of the Holocaust from the sharply delineated perspective of the "damaged life" and the barbarity and totalitarianism of the age. Do you see yourself as the heir to this no longer subterranean current?

J. H.: Well, Adorno understood his own critique of the reification of interpersonal relationships and psychic impulses as an implication of the prohibition against images [*Bilderverbot*]. Reification is a worshiping of idols, the inversion of the conditioned into the unconditioned. Negative-dialectical thought is supposed to rescue the non-identical in things which are violated by our abstractions. It is supposed to restore the integrity of the individual which has been mutilated by unavoidable subsumption. Adorno's reflections are guided by the intuition that a subjectivity run amok that objectifies everything around it elevates itself into an absolute, and thereby violates the true absolute, the unconditional right of each creature to recognition and respect for its integrity. The rage of objectification overlooks the essential core of the fully individuated other which makes the creature into the "image of God."

Viewed philosophically, the powerful cognitive advance of the "Axial Age"[2] is captured in the First Commandment, namely, emancipation from the chain of kinship and from the arbitrariness of mythic powers. At that time, the major world religions, as they developed a monotheistic or acosmic concept of the absolute, pierced through the uniform, smooth surface of contingent appearances interwoven by narrative, and broke open the chasm between deep and surface structure, between essence and appearance, which first conferred the freedom of reflection and the power to distance oneself from the giddy multiplicity of immediacy. For these concepts of the absolute or the unconditioned inaugurate the distinction between logical and empirical relations, validity and genesis, truth and health, guilt and causality, law and violence, and so forth. This marks the emergence of the constellation of concepts which still informed the preoccupations of German idealism: the relation between the infinite and the finite, the unconditioned and the conditioned, unity and multiplicity, freedom and necessity.

Only after Hegel, with the Young Hegelians and Nietzsche, did this constellation undergo a further shift. But this "postmetaphysical" thought has remained deeply ambiguous. To this day it continues to be threatened by the possibility of regression into "neopaganism." The young conservative forerunners of fascism in the early 1930s used this term to describe their project, inspired by Hölderlin and Nietzsche, of recovering the archaic sources of the pre-Socratics, the "origins" which precede the threshold of monotheism and the Platonic logos. In his posthumously published *Spiegel* interview, Heidegger was still using this polytheistic jargon: "Only a god can save us. . . ." In the wake of the postmodernist critique of reason, these neopagan figures of thought have become fashionable again. Such metaphors as "networks," "family resemblances," "rhizomes," and so on may initially have had the unobjectionable pragmatic meaning of sharpening our sensitivity for contexts. But in the context of Nietzsche's and Heidegger's critique of metaphysics, they acquire the connotation of a rejection of the universalistic meaning of unconditional validity claims. Adorno bristled against this regressive tendency within postmetaphysical thought when he vowed to keep faith with metaphysics "at the moment of its downfall." Following Nietzsche, he was more concerned with deepening the dialectical criticism of the "logic of essences" than with the superficial anti-Platonism which is today spreading so mindlessly in the fashionable penumbra of the late Heidegger and the late Wittgenstein. In this intention, if not in the means of realizing it, I am in complete agreement with Adorno.

Question: It is clear that the points of departure for the second generation of the Frankfurt School were and remain different: the Cold War, the defense of democracy, the preservation and furthering of the hard-won gains of the Enlightenment, the critique of new forms of reification and commodification, the discovery of the civilizing role of law, the overcoming of the philosophy of consciousness, etc. But hasn't religion, in whatever form, ceased to provide impulses for your development of critical theory?

J. H.: I can't speak for the "second generation," only for myself – or perhaps also for Karl-Otto Apel – in what I am about to say. I would not object if someone were to say that my conception of language and my communicative concept of action oriented to reaching understanding are nourished by the legacy of Christianity. The "telos of reaching understanding" – the idea of discursively achieved agreement which measures itself against the standard of intersubjective recognition, hence the double negation of criticizable validity claims – may well draw on the legacy of the Christian understanding of the logos which is, after all, embodied in the communicative practice of religious congregations (and not just the Quakers). Already the communicative-theoretical conception of emancipation in *Knowledge and Human Interests*[3] could be "unmasked" as the secularized translation of the promise of salvation. (However, in the meantime I have become more cautious about using the expression "emancipation" outside the domain of individual life histories, since social collectives, groups, and communities cannot be regarded as subjects writ large.) I only mean to say that the proof of theological antecedents does not bother me, as long as the methodological difference between discourses remains clear, that is, as long as philosophical discourse remains answerable to the distinctive demands of justificatory speech. In my view, a philosophy that oversteps the limits of methodological atheism forfeits its philosophical seriousness.

By the way, one teaching drawn from Jakob Böhme's mystical speculations on the emergence of "nature" through a process of contraction, or the "dark ground" in God, was very important for me. Later, Gershom Scholem drew my attention to its counterpart, namely, Isaac Luria's doctrine of *zimzum*.[4] Interestingly, these two speculative ideas, which developed independently, were brought together, via Knorr von Rosenheim and Schwabian Pietism, in the thought of Baader and Schelling, and post-Fichtean idealism in general. In the essay on freedom already mentioned and in his philosophy of the "Ages of the World," Schelling drew on this tradition and located the tension-laden relation between "egoity" and "love" in God Himself. This "dark" tendency toward finitization [*Verendlichung*] or contraction is intended as an explanation of God's capacity for self-limitation. I have dealt with this already in my doctoral dissertation.

The problem concerns the decisive moment of the creation of the first Adam which brings to a close the era of ideal creation, which, like the movement of Hegel's "logic," took place only in the mind or God. In order to confirm his own freedom through an alter ego, God must set limits to this very freedom. Thus he equips Adam *kadmos*[5] with the unconditional freedom of good and evil, and thereby accepts the risk that Adam may make the wrong use of this gift by sinning and dragging the whole of ideal creation down with him into the abyss. He would thus topple God himself from his throne. As we know, this "worst case scenario" is precisely what happened. The story solves the problem of theodicy, but at the cost of inaugurating a new world era, the age of world history, with this terrible act of freedom. In the second, historical age, a humbled God must himself await redemption, because humanity has taken upon itself the burden of resurrecting fallen nature.

This myth – and this is why it is more than just a myth – illuminates two aspects of human freedom: the intersubjective constitution of autonomy and the meaning of the self-binding of the individual will to unconditionally valid norms.

The creation of the first human can only have this catastrophic consequence because the act of creation conducted, so to speak, *in mente* must start all over again from the beginning of history. For no subject, not even God Himself, can be truly free unless he is recognized as free by at least one other subject, that is, by someone who is free in the same sense (and who is, in turn, in need of reciprocal recognition). No one can enjoy freedom alone or at the cost of the freedom of someone else. Thus freedom may never be conceived merely negatively, as the absence of compulsion. The intersubjective conception of freedom differs from the arbitrary freedom of the isolated individual. No one is free until we all are free. The second aspect of freedom, the unconditioned character of the moral ought, is underlined by the fact that the fate of God and the world as a whole stands in balance with the good and evil that historically acting subjects mutually ascribe to one another. Human beings feel the full weight of the categorical ought in the superhuman responsibility for an inverted history of salvation. Inserted as authors into such a highly charged world history, they must answer to it as before a Last Judgment that remains stubbornly beyond their control.

Question: Let me be more direct. In your essay "Reflections on a Remark of Max Horkheimer," you write in conclusion: "It may perhaps be said that to seek to salvage an unconditional meaning without God is a futile undertaking, for it belongs to the peculiar dignity of philosophy to maintain adamantly that no validity claim can have cognitive import unless it is vindicated before the tribunal of justificatory discourse."[6] Your aim in writing this was to differentiate the philosophical meaning of "unconditionality" from the unconditionality of the religious promise of salvation, which offers consolation in the face of suffering, defeat, and a misspent life. "Unconditionality" in the philosophical sense is grounded in the quest for truth and to this extent is, or should be, postmetaphysical. But elsewhere you write: "Philosophy, even in its postmetaphysical form, will be able neither to replace nor to repress religion as long as religious language is the bearer of a semantic content that is inspiring and even indispensable, for this content eludes (for the time being?) the explanatory force of philosophical language and continues to resist translation into reasoning discourses."[7] These two quotations reveal two conflicting tendencies in your work: either religion is dissolved into communicative reason and assimilated to discourse ethics, or religion is ascribed the function of preserving, and even nurturing, semantic contents which are indispensable for ethics and morality, indeed for philosophy as such.

J. H.: I see no contradiction here. In the confrontation with Horkheimer I only wanted to show that the concept of unconditioned truth can be defended not just with strong theological assumptions but also under the more modest premises of postmetaphysical thinking. The second quotation, by contrast, expresses the conviction that indispensable semantic potentials are preserved in religious language, potentials that philosophy has not yet fully exhausted by translating them into the language of public reasons, that is, reasons assumed to be capable of commanding general agreement. Taking the example of the concept of the individual person, which the language of monotheistic religions has articulated from the outset with all the precision one could wish for, I attempted to point out this deficit, or at least the clumsiness of philosophical attempts at translation. In my view, the basic concepts of philosophical ethics, as they have been developed up to this point, do not even come close to capturing all the intuitions which already found nuanced expression in the language of the Bible and which we learn only through a halfway religious socialization. Mindful of this deficiency, discourse ethics attempts to translate the categorical imperative into a language that enables us to do justice to another intuition, I mean the feeling of "solidarity," the bond of a member of a community to her fellow members.

Question: I will return to this point. But let us remain with the second quotation for a moment. You add "for the time being?" in parentheses. Is it your view that the goal of philosophy is to assimilate, to translate, to rework and to "sublate" all religious contents worth preserving? Or do you expect that religion will indefinitely resist all such attempted interventions, and that it will therefore remain forever inassimilable and inaccessible, and to a certain extent also autonomous and indispensable?

J. H.: I don't know. That will transpire when philosophy conducts its work on its religious heritage with more sensitivity than heretofore. I don't mean the neopagan project of a "work on myth" which has long since been completed by religion and theology.

Question: The relationship between religion and theology is not unlike that between the lifeworld and philosophy. Thus, as the horizon of the lifeworld retreats ever further with every advance made by philosophical explanation, religion retreats with every serious attempt of theology to advance into the inner realms of religious experience. Could it be that the contradictory attitudes toward religion that strike me in your work stem from a conflation of religion and theology?

J. H.: I see what you are driving at. Theology would forfeit its identity if it attempted to detach itself from religion's dogmatic core and hence from the religious language in which a religious community's practices of prayer, confession, and faith unfold. These are the practices in which religious faith, which theology can only interpret, proves itself. Theology already has a certain parasitic or derivative status. It cannot disguise the fact that its interpretive work can never entirely "recover" or "exhaust" the performative meaning of lived faith. Now you will say that this is all the more true of philosophy! Perhaps philosophy can "purloin" a few concepts from theology (as Benjamin put it in his "Theses on the Philosophy of History"), but it would be the worst kind of intellectualism to expect that philosophy could more or less completely appropriate the forms of experience preserved in religious language along the "path of translation."

In one sense, however, this is a false comparison. Theology cannot provide a substitute for religion, for the latter's truth is nourished by the revealed Word, which inherently manifests itself in religious and not in learned form. But philosophy has an entirely different relation to religion. It seeks to express what it can learn from religion in a discourse that is marked precisely by its independence from revealed truth. Thus, every philosophical translation, even Hegel's, forfeits the performative meaning of lived faith. A philosophy that makes itself dependent on, or takes solace from, "destinies" [*Geschicke*] is no longer philosophy. The goal of philosophy's "translation program" is, if you like, to rescue at most the profane meaning of interpersonal and existential experiences that have thus far only been adequately articulated in religious language. In contemporary terms, I am thinking of responses to extreme situations of helplessness, of the loss of self, or of the threat of annihilation, which leave us "at a loss for words."

Question: In many places you have argued that "solidarity" and "justice" are two sides of the same coin. More recently, you have even tried to trace this idea to the core of Christian faith.[8] But doesn't the specifically Christian meaning of love or solidarity mean more than equal respect, namely, a form of concern for others that goes beyond any claim to justice, equal treatment, or the fair distribution of burdens and benefits? God is what is "completely other" and this otherness announces itself in the strict negation of the suffering of others. This other of the divine epiphany enjoins us to a form of action beyond all calculation and "triangulation." This idea can be discerned in the appeals of third world liberation theologians when they call for solidarity with the victims of the brutal process of modernization. The priority enjoyed by "sympathy with the poor" expresses the Christian priority of solidarity over justice. It is in a sense more original than justice.

J. H.: Yes, the ethic of Christian love does justice to an aspect of devotion to suffering others that receives short shrift in an intersubjectively conceived morality of justice. The latter limits itself to the justification of commands that each ought to follow on the condition that they are also followed by all others. However, there is a good reason for this self-limitation. A supererogatory act that goes beyond what can be reasonably expected of everyone on the basis of reciprocity amounts to the active sacrifice of one's own legitimate interests for the wellbeing, or the reduction of the suffering, of others in need of help. The imitation of Christ enjoins even such an inordinate sacrifice on the believer, on the condition, of course, that she freely assumes this active sacrifice which is sanctified by a just and good God and an absolute Judge. But there is no absolute power on earth. Here in our sublunary realm, the Christian injunction to love one's neighbor has often been abused for fateful purposes and false sacrifices. No earthly power may impose a sacrifice upon an autonomous individual for supposedly higher ends. This is why the Enlightenment wanted to abolish sacrifice. Today, this same skepticism is directed against the death penalty and against the legitimacy of obligatory military service. This is the reason for the cautiously resigned restriction to a morality of justice. This does not diminish our admiration for absolute devotion to one's neighbor, and certainly not our respect, indeed admiration, for all those unspectacular, selfless sacrifices, mostly by mothers and women, without which the last

moral bond would have long since been broken in many pathologi-
cally distorted societies (and not just there).

Question: I would like to press you on this issue. I am thinking of
the type of criticisms repeatedly made by people like Gutierrez, Boff,
and Dussel. The standard of living of the greater part of the world's
population is so miserable that, in comparison with OECD countries,
symmetry, reciprocity, and reversibility represent false standards for
morally judging and combating this drastic gap. Moreover, equal
treatment is an unattainable goal already for ecological reasons. For
the liberation theologians and philosophers, therefore, a moral theory
that stops at the abstract equality of the "moral point of view" is
merely a luxury of the exceptional circumstances enjoyed by the
wealthy nations of the developed world. The normal condition in all
other countries is one of extreme privation and inhuman living conditions. The standpoint of reciprocity cannot do justice to this situation. We are called upon to do more than can be justified on the
basis of obligations deriving from contractual agreements among presumptive equals. Global responsibility today calls for a commitment
that goes far beyond that to which we are morally obligated. This is
what the liberation theologians mean when they speak of the "pref-
erential option for the poor."

J. H.: I will leave aside the distinction between Kantianism and con-
tractualism and will also not rely on the objection that the standards
of so-called "abstract justice," if they were only applied, would be
entirely adequate to revolutionize global society. Just imagine for
a moment that the G-7 states were to assume global responsibility
and agree on policies that met John Rawls's (contractualistically
grounded) second principle of justice: "social and economic inequalities are to be arranged so that it can be reasonably expected to be
of the greatest benefit to the least advantaged." To be sure, the unjust
global distribution of the benefits of good fortune has always been a
central preoccupation of the major world religions. But, in a secularized society, this problem must first be placed on the political and
economic table, not shoved immediately into the cupboard of morality, let alone of moral theory.

What is the scandal? In a world still dominated by nation-states,
there is still no regime capable of political action which could assume
the "global responsibility" demanded by moral points of view. And

existing interest positions are no more encouraging for the spontaneous formation of a countervailing political will capable of implementing a corresponding "moral division of labor" between the
various members of an intolerably stratified world society. The
burning issue of a more just global economic order poses itself in
the first instance as a political problem. How a democratically
responsible politics can catch up with runaway globalized markets is,
in any event, not a question for moral theory; social scientists and
economists have more to offer here than philosophers. At the analytical level, it calls for a great deal of empirical knowledge and institutional imagination. In the final analysis, of course, even the best
designs are of no help unless political processes come into play. At
the practical level, only social movements will be able to generate
the necessary motivations across national borders.

The outcry of liberation theology in its quest to lend a voice to
the miserable and the downtrodden, the oppressed and the humiliated, does indeed stand within this context. I understand it as active
outrage over the inertia and insensitivity of a *status quo* that seems
to be frozen in the vortex of a self-propelling modernization process.
The "more" of its brave, self-sacrificing commitment, which extends
far beyond what can be reasonably expected, is justified by its participants through the Christian command to love. Viewed from
another angle, however, the supererogatory character of this personal
initiative also appears as a reflex of the powerlessness of the individual, however admirable, in the face of the anonymous, systemic
constraints of politically untamed capitalism which only understands
the language of prices, but not that of morality.

Question: When we look back over the twentieth century and
attempt to give an account of what happened, we cannot help but
agree with Hobsbawm that it was a century of extremes. Some might
want to add that it was a century of radical evil. There is something
profoundly inexcusable and unacceptable in what transpired during
the twentieth century. What can we learn from this "radical evil"? Is
there any lesson to be learnt?

J. H.: The Holocaust was unimaginable up to the very moment it
began; thus radical evil also has a historical index. By this I mean that
there is a peculiar asymmetry between the knowledge of good and
of evil. We know what we should not do, what we must absolutely

refrain from doing, if we want to be able to look ourselves in the face without blushing. But we don't know what human beings are ultimately capable of. And the more evil increases, the stronger is the apparent need to repress and forget incurred guilt. This is the depressing experience of my adult political life in Germany. But I have also had the good fortune of having another experience, which at least gives me hope that Richard Rorty is not entirely wrong when he, as an American, says what I would perhaps not express with the same degree of self-confidence: "Nothing a nation has done should make it impossible for (citizens of) a constitutional democracy to regain self-respect."

Notes

Chapter 1 There are Alternatives!

1 During the 1980s, Kohl initiated a shift toward a more conservative mentality and cultural climate following the left-liberal administrations under Willy Brandt and Helmut Schmidt. At that time, the shift was popularly known as "*die Wende*" (i.e. "the Turn"), though this term is now used to refer to the post-1989 reunification process. (*Eds.*)

2 On September 5, 1977 the Red Army Faction (RAF) abducted and later murdered the industrialist Hans Martin Schleyer in Cologne. The socialist-liberal coalition government under Helmut Schmidt responded to the abduction and a subsequent airplane hijacking with harsh security measures, contributing to an atmosphere of crisis and instability. (*Eds.*)

3 Gustav Heinemann (1899–1976) was president of the Federal Republic from 1969 to 1974. A co-founder of the conservative CDU party, he served as interior minister in the first government of Konrad Adenauer before resigning in 1950 over Adenauer's policy of rearming the Bundeswehr. He later joined the Social Democratic party (SPD). As Bundespräsident, he supported Willy Brandt's policy of *rapprochement* with the Eastern Bloc and won considerable national and international respect for his stances on constitutional questions and issues relating to the Nazi past. (*Eds.*)

4 Oskar Lafontaine is a prominent German left-wing politician, a former chairman of the SPD and its unsuccessful chancellor candidate in the 1990 federal elections. He served as finance minister in the first Red-Green coalition government before resigning abruptly in 1999 following sharp differences with Gerhard Schröder and other members of the cabinet over economic policy. Since then, he has been a vocal critic of Schröder's social and economic policies and has candidated unsuccessfully as leader of a new left-wing party, The Left. (*Eds.*)

5 Theo Waigel was the leader of the Bavarian "sister party" of the CDU, the Christian Social Union (CSU), from 1988 to 1999 and served as finance minister under Helmut Kohl from 1989 to 1998. (*Eds.*)

6 Following World War II, the East German government tore down the remains of the Berlin Stadtschloss – i.e. the "City Castle," the former palace and seat of government of the Prussian Hohenzollern dynasty – and erected a modern building, the Palace of the Republic, on the site. Since this interview took place, the Federal Parliament has passed a resolution to demolish the Palace of the Republic, and a number of civic initiatives are being organized to raise money to re-erect a replica of the old baroque palace. In the meantime, the Memorial to the Murdered Jews of Europe has been completed near the Brandenburg Gate in the center of Berlin and was officially opened on May 10, 2005. (On the controversy surrounding the Memorial, see below chs. 4 and 5.) (*Eds.*)

Chapter 2 From Power Politics to Cosmopolitan Society

1 In addition to his position as Vice-Chancellor, Joschka Fischer (The Greens) was German Foreign Minister from 1998 until 2005. Rudolf Scharping (SPD), Minister of Defense from 1998 until his dismissal in 2001 following a series of political gaffes, was a major advocate of German participation in the NATO intervention in Kosovo, the first postwar combat operation of the Bundeswehr. (*Eds.*)

2 Alfred Dregger (1920–2002) was a prominent member of the CDU and a vocal anti-communist and supporter of conservative-nationalist causes; Egon Bahr (SPD) held various cabinet positions under Willy Brandt and Helmut Schmidt and opposed Schmidt's policy of stationing nuclear missiles in Germany; Hans-Christian Stroeble is a Member of Parliament for the Greens who has supported pacifist causes throughout his political career; Volker Rühe (CDU) was Defense Minister under Helmut Kohl from 1992 to 1998; Wolfgang Schäuble (CDU) held various cabinet posts under Helmut Kohl and prominent positions within the CDU until he was tainted by the donations scandal (see ch. 4), though he remains a prominent figure within the party; Erhard Eppler (SPD) was a member of cabinet under Kiesinger, Brandt, and Schmidt and has been a prominent supporter of the peace and environmental movements since the 1980s. (*Eds.*)

3 The nineteenth-century German poet and political activist Ernst-Morris Arndt (1769–1860) defended a virulently chauvinistic form of German nationalism. Hans Jakob Christoph von Grimmelshausen (1621–76) was the author of the first prose novel in the German language, *Simplicissimus* (1669). (*Eds.*)

Chapter 3 A Sort of Logo of the Free West

1 Kiep was arrested in November 1999 in relation to a large undeclared
   political donation from an arms manufacturer. Subsequent criminal
   investigations and parliamentary commissions revealed that the CDU
   had maintained a secret system of foreign bank accounts and foundations over decades into which presumably illegal donations were chan-
   neled as a political slush fund under the personal control of Helmut
   Kohl. Kohl publicly admitted receiving undeclared contributions, but
   has steadfastly refused to reveal the names of the donors, citing his personal "word of honor" to preserve their anonymity. The federal CDU
   suffered serious financial penalties when the existence of the undeclared contributions became public, and among the political repercus-
   sions of the scandal were the resignation of then chairman Wolfgang
   Schäuble and the rise of his successor Angela Merkel, who was the first
   prominent member of the party to criticize Kohl publicly. In January
   2000, the CDU party in the state of Hesse was drawn into the scandal
   when it emerged that, from 1983 onwards, the head of the party (and
   subsequent federal Interior Minister) Manfred Kanther, the financial
   advisor Horst Weyrauch, and the party treasurer had sequestered illegal
   donations in foreign bank accounts under the guise of "Jewish bequests."
   The scandal rocked the state government in Wiesbaden and tainted the
   CDU Minister President Roland Koch, though, like Kohl, he has survived relatively unscathed. (*Eds.*)
2 Edmund Stoiber is Minister President of the State of Bavaria and the
   leader of the conservative Bavarian "sister party" of the CDU, the CSU.
   (*Eds.*)
3 The Flick affair in the early 1980s concerned illegal political donations
   to a range of political parties by the Flick industrial concern, which had
   been a major employer of slave labor under the Nazis, with the intention of creating a favorable political climate for its extensive business
   interests. The scandal revealed an urgent need for tighter legal regulation of party funding. (*Eds.*)

Chapter 4 The Finger of Blame: The Germans and Their Memorial

1 The German novelist Martin Walser caused a controversy when, in a
   speech in the Paulskirche in Frankfurt on October 11, 1998, he complained of the "permanent presentation of our shame in the media" and
   implied that it was time to draw a line under the Nazi past. (*Eds.*)
2 The Reichstag building was renovated by the West German government
   during the 1970s in anticipation of the eventual unification of the two
   Germanys and duly became the home of the Federal Parliament (the

"Bundestag") following the move from Bonn to Berlin (completed in 2000–1). The name "Reichstag" (lit. "Imperial Parliament") evokes memories of the aggressive militarism of the Wilhelmine era and the rise to power of the Nazis. (*Eds.*)

3 Phillip Jenninger (CDU) was president of the Bundestag from 1984 to 1988. He had to resign following a well-meaning but ill-judged speech to Parliament to mark the fiftieth anniversary of Kristallnacht. (*Eds.*)

4 Hans Globke (1898–1973) was one of the authors of the Nuremberg race laws and had a successful career in the CDU after the war. He became advisor to Chancellor Konrad Adenauer in 1953, a powerful position which he held for ten years in spite of public knowledge of his Nazi past. The actor and director Veit Harlan (1899–1964) had a successful career under the Nazis as a director of feature films with pronounced propagandistic and, in the case of *Jud Süss* (1940), anti-Semitic content. Otto John (1909–97), a participant in the plot to assassinate Hitler in 1944, became director of the West German secret service in 1950. His apparent defection (and possible kidnapping) to East Germany in 1954 caused a furore and, following his voluntary return to the West in 1955, he was convicted of treason and sentenced to four years in prison. (*Eds.*)

5 In this essay, Habermas uses three related German words in connection with the Memorial – *Denkmal*, *Schandmal*, and *Mahnmal* – whose lexical relation to the root "*Mal*" (lit. "mole" or "mark," as in "birthmark" or "mark of Cain") is difficult to render straightforwardly in English. *Mahnmal*, which means a memorial intended as a warning (from *mahnen*, to warn or exhort), does not have an exact English equivalent and is generally translated simply as "memorial," though in one place we have used "admonition" to highlight its specific monitory connotation. It is worth noting that, although the official title of the Holocaust Memorial is *Denkmal*, it is commonly referred to as the *Holocaust Mahnmal*. (*Eds.*)

6 In his dramatic painting of the crucifixion on the Isenheim Altarpiece (Musée d'Unterlinden, Colmar), Matthias Grünewald (1470–1528) depicts John the Baptist holding scriptures in his left hand while pointing to the crucified Christ with his right. Although the precise devotional context for which the complex altarpiece was produced is a matter of conjecture and it predates the Reformation (the paintings were completed in 1516), John the Baptist's gesture has been interpreted as an expression of the Lutheran view of the crucifixion as a symbol of human guilt and shame. (*Eds.*)

7 Hermann Lübbe is a prominent liberal-conservative political philosopher who has taken controversial positions on postwar German political controversies. On Rudolf Augstein, see below, ch. 10, n. 3. On Martin Walser, see above, n. 1. (*Eds.*)

8 Dubiel, *Niemand ist frei von der Geschichte* (Munich: Carl Hanser, 1999), p. 292.

9 The Neue Wache (lit. "New Guardhouse") originally served as a barracks for the royal guard from 1818 to 1918 and later as a memorial to the war dead of World War I, and, under the East German regime, to "the victims of fascism and militarism." It was rededicated in 1993 as the "Central Memorial of the Federal Republic of Germany for the Victims of War and Dictatorship" through a personal initiative of Chancellor Helmut Kohl. The neoclassical building in the center of Berlin contains a massive enlargement of a 1914 statue by Käthe Kollwitz dedicated to the "victims of war and violence" depicting a mother and her fallen son in a variation on the traditional *pietà* motif. Kohl's initiative drew hefty criticism from the historian Reinhart Koselleck, who argued that the Kollwitz statue lent the memorial an anti-Jewish character by evoking the Christian anti-Semitism traditionally associated with the commemoration of the death of Christ. (*Eds.*)

10 The German-Jewish philosopher and logician Hermann Cohen (1842–1918) defended a rationalist-universalist interpretation of the Jewish religious tradition. (*Eds.*)

Chapter 5 Symbolic Expression and Ritualistic Behavior

1 In Germany, resistance to the Nazis is commemorated on July 20 (recollecting the attempted assassination of Hitler on July 20, 1944) and the fall of the Berlin Wall on November 9. (*Eds.*)

2 See ch. 4, n. 9. (*Eds.*)

3 G. W. F. Hegel, *Jenaer Systementwürfe I*, fragment 22 (Hamburg: Meiner, 1986), p. 224.

4 Ernst Cassirer, *An Essay on Man* (New Haven: Yale University Press, 1945), p. 25.

5 On what follows, see Habermas, "Die befreiende Kraft der symbolischen Formgebung," in *Vom sinnlichen Eindruck zum symbolischen Ausdruck* (Frankfurt am Main: Suhrkamp, 1997), pp. 9–40.

6 Ernst Cassirer, *Naturalistische und humanistische Begründung der Kulturphilosophie* (Göteborg: Elanders Boktryckeri Aktiebolag, 1939), p. 16.

7 Ernst Cassirer, *Die Idee der Republikanischen Verfassung* (Hamburg, 1929), p. 31.

8 Arnold Gehlen, *Urmensch und Spätkultur* (Bonn, 1956), p. 178.

9 Ibid., p. 9.

10 Arnold Gehlen, *Die Seele im technischen Zeitalter* (Hamburg, 1957), p. 118.

11 Gehlen, *Urmensch und Spätkultur*, p. 233.

12 Ibid., p. 65.

13 Ibid., p. 91.

14 Gehlen, "Mensch und Institutionen," in *Anthropologische und Sozialpsychologische Untersuchungen* (Hamburg: Rowohlt, 1986), pp. 69–77, esp. p. 77.

15 Jürgen Habermas, *Theory of Communicative Action*, trans. Thomas McCarthy (Boston: Beacon Press, 1987), vol. II, pp. 43–111.

Chapter 6 Euroskepticism, Market Europe, or a Europe of (World) Citizens?

1 Richard Münch, *Globale Dynamik, locale Lebenswelten: Der schwierige Weg in die Weltgesellschaft* (Frankfurt am Main: Suhrkamp, 1998).

2 Robert Cox, "Economic Globalization and the Limits to Liberal Democracy," in Anthony G. McGrew (ed.), *The Transformation of Democracy?* (London: The Open University Press, 1997), pp. 49–72.

3 David Held, Anthony G. McGrew, David Goldblatt, and Jonathan Perraton, *Global Transformations* (Cambridge: Polity, 1999). See also Held and McGrew (eds.), *The Global Transformations Reader* (Cambridge: Polity, 2000).

4 Lothar Brock, "Die Grenzen der Demokratie: Selbstbestimmung im Kontext des globalen Strukturwandels," in Beata Kohler-Koch (ed.), *Regieren in entgrenzten Räume* (Politische Vierteljahresschrift, Sonderheft 29, 1998), pp. 271–92.

5 David Held, *Democracy and the Global Order* (Cambridge: Polity, 1995), pp. 99ff.

6 Michael Zürn, "Gesellschaftliche Denationalisierung und Regieren in der OECD-Welt," in Kohler-Koch (ed.), *Regieren in entgrenzten Räume*, pp. 91–120.

7 Fritz W. Scharpf maintains that the results of intergovernmental negotiations, given the veto power of each member, have "their own basis of legitimacy in the norm that all participants must consent to decisions and that none will if, on balance, they would be worse off than if the negotiations were to fail." Scharpf, "Demokratie in der transnationalen Politik," in Ulrich Beck (ed.), *Politik der Globalisierung* (Frankfurt am Main: Suhrkamp, 1998), p. 237. This argument can justify neither the derivative nor the reduced character of such legitimation, that is, neither the fact that supranational agreements are not subject to the legitimation pressures of national arenas to the same extent as domestic decisions, nor the fact that the process of will-formation institutionalized at the level of the nation-state is also guided by intersubjectively recognized norms and values and is not reducible to a process of pure compromise, that is, a rational-choice balancing of interests. Of course, it is no more possible to trace the deliberative politics of citizens and their representatives back to expert knowledge. See the justi-

fication of the "European comitology" advanced by Christian Joerges and Jürgen Neyer, "Von intergouvernementalem Verhandeln zur deliberativen Politik," in Kohler-Koch (ed.), *Regieren in entgrenzten Räume*, pp. 207–34.

8 Wolfgang Streeck (ed.), *Internationale Wirtschaft, nationale Demokratie* (Frankfurt am Main: Campus, 1998), pp. 19f.

9 See Jürgen Habermas, *The Postnational Constellation: Political Essays*, ed. and trans. Max Pensky (Cambridge: Polity, 2001), pp. 58ff.

10 Streeck (ed.), *Internationale Wirtschaft, nationale Demokratie*, p. 38.

11 Anthony Giddens, *The Third Way: The Renewal of Social Democracy* (Cambridge: Polity, 1988), p. 100; see also Joshua Cohen and Joel Rogers, "Can Egalitarianism Survive Internationalization?," in Streeck (ed.), *Internationale Wirtschaft, nationale Demokratie*, pp. 175–94.

12 Zukunftskommission der Friedrich Ebert Stiftung (eds.), *Wirtschaftliche Leistungsfähigkeit, sozialer Zusammenhalt und ökologische Nachhaltigkeit* (Bonn: Dietz, 1998), pp. 225ff.

13 On this terminology, see Jürgen Habermas, "On the Pragmatic, Moral, and Ethical Uses of Reason," in *Justification and Application: Remarks on Discourse Ethics*, trans. Ciaran Cronin (Cambridge: Polity, 1993), pp. 1–18.

14 Thomas Maak and York Lunau (eds.), *Weltwirtschaftsethik* (Bern: Paul Haupt, 1998), p. 24.

15 Ulrich Thielemann, "Globale Konkurrenz, Sozialstandards, und der Zwang zum Unternehmertum," in Maak and Lunau (eds.), *Weltwirtschaftsethik*, p. 231.

16 Peter Ulrich, *Integrative Wirtschaftsethik* (Bern: Paul Haupt, 1997), p. 334.

17 Eugen Richter, "Demokratie und Globalisierung," in Ansgar Klein and Rainer Schmalz-Bruns, *Politische Beteiligung und Bürgerengagement in Deutschland* (Baden-Baden: Nomos, 1997), pp. 173–202.

18 Wolfgang Streeck, "Vom Binnenmarkt zum Bundesstaat?," in Stephan Leibfried and Paul Pierson (eds.), *Standort Europa* (Frankfurt am Main: Suhrkamp, 1998), pp. 369–421.

19 Hans Tietmeyer was president of the Deutsche Bundesbank, the German central bank (not to be confused with the commercial Deutsche Bank mentioned in the following paragraph) from 1993 to 1999. (*Eds.*)

20 Rolf E. Breuer, "Offene Bürgergesellschaft in der globalisierten Weltwirtschaft," *Frankfurter Allgemeine Zeitung* (January 4, 1999), p. 9.

21 *Ibid.*

22 Claus Offe, "Demokratie und Wohlfahrtsstaat: Eine europäische Regimeform under dem Stress der europäische Integration," in Streeck (ed.), *Internationale Wirtschaft, nationale Demokratie*, pp. 99–136.

23   Dieter Grimm, *Braucht Europa eine Verfassung?* (Munich: Carl-Friedrich-von-Siemens-Stiftung, 1995); on this, see Habermas, *The Inclusion of the Other: Essays in Political Theory,* ed. and trans. Ciaran Cronin and Pablo De Greiff (Cambridge: Polity, 1998), pp. 155–64.

24   Klaus Eder, Kai-Uwe Hellmann, and Hans-Jörg Trenz, "Regieren in Europa jenseits öffentlicher Legitimation?," in Kohler-Koch (ed.), *Regieren in entgrenzten Räume,* pp. 321–44.

25   See the introduction and essays in Part 4 of Maak and Lunau (eds.), *Weltwirtschaftsethik.*

26   Habermas, *The Postnational Constellation,* pp. 58ff.

Chapter 7 Does Europe Need a Constitution?

1   Frank Niess, *Die europäische Idee* (Frankfurt am Main: Suhrkamp, 2001).

2   Niess, "Das 'F-Wort'," in *Blätter für deutsche und internationale Politik* (September 2000), pp. 1105–15.

3   Larry Siedentop, *Democracy in Europe* (London: Allen Lane, 2000), p. 1.

4   *The Debate on the Constitution,* vols. 1 & 2 (New York: Library of America, 1993).

5   See above pp. 27–8.

6   See John E. Fossum, "Constitution-making in the European Union," in John E. Fossum and Erik O. Erikson (eds.), *Democracy in the European Union: Integration through Deliberation?* (London: Routledge, 2000), pp. 11–163.

7   Lionel Jospin, speech to the Foreign Press Association, Paris, May 28, 2001.

8   On the following, see Georg Vobruba, *Alternativen zur Vollbeschäftigung* (Frankfurt am Main: Suhrkamp, 2001).

9   Göran Therborn, "Europe's Break with Itself," in Furio Cerutti and Enno Rudoph (eds.), *A Soul for Europe: On the Political and Cultural Identity of the Europeans,* vol. 2 (Sterling, VA: Peters Leuven, 2001), pp. 44–56, here p. 52.

10   See ch. 6, above.

11   Edgar Grande and Thomas Risse, "Bridging the Gap," *Zeitschrift für internationale Beziehungen* (October 2000), pp. 235–66.

12   Josef Esser, "Der kooperative Nationalstaat im Zeitalter der 'Globalisierung'," in Dieter Döring (ed.), *Sozialstaat in der Globalisierung* (Frankfurt am Main: Campus, 1999), pp. 117–44.

13   Fritz W. Scharpf, "The Viability of Advanced Welfare States in the International Economy," *Journal of European Public Policy,* 7 (2000), pp. 190–228.

14   *Die Zeit* (June 7, 2001).

15 Mario Telò and Paul Mignette, "Justice and Solidarity," in Cerutti and Rudolph (eds.), *A Soul for Europe*, vol. 1, p. 51.

16 Georg Vobruba, "Die Erweiterungskrise der Europäische Union," *Leviathan*, 28 (2000), pp. 477–96.

17 Jospin (2001): "The most urgent task is the combat against 'social dumping'; for it is unacceptable for some member states to use unfair taxation competition to lure global investments and entice European companies to relocate their headquarters there."

18 Claus Offe, "Is There, or Can There be a 'European Society'?" in Ines Katenhusen and Wolfram Lamping (eds.), *Demokratien in Europa* (Opladen: Leske and Budrick, 2002).

19 See Ernst-Wolfgang Böckenförde, *Welchen Weg geht Europa?* (Munich: C. F. von Siemens-Stiftung, 1997).

20 This is the title of an empirical analysis by Philip Schlesinger and Deirdre Kevin in Fossum and Erikson (eds.), *Democracy in the European Union*, pp. 206–29.

21 Prior to May 1, 2004, the 15 EU member states had 13 official languages between them, 11 of which were official working languages of the EU (the two exceptions being Irish and Luxembourgish). With the eastward enlargement in 2004, the EU acquired 9 additional official and working languages. (*Eds.*)

22 Peter Kraus, "Von Westfalen nach Kosmopolis. Die Problematik kultureller Identität in der Europäischen Politik," *Berliner Journal für Soziologie*, 2 (2000), pp. 203–18; and "Political Unity and Linguistic Diversity in Europe," *Archives Européennes de Sociologie*, 41 (2000), pp. 138–63.

23 Kraus cites a survey finding that already a majority of the German-speaking Swiss prefer English to the two other national languages for communication across linguistic boundaries.

24 Pim den Boer, "Europe as an Idea," *European Review*, 6 (October 1998), pp. 395–402.

25 Reinhold Viehoff and Rien T. Segers (eds.), *Kultur, Identität, Europa* (Frankfurt am Main: Suhrkamp, 1999).

26 Therborn, "Europe's Break with Itself," in Cerutti and Rudoph (eds.), *A Soul for Europe*, vol. 2, pp. 49f.

27 The Convention, which was assigned the task of drafting the Charter by the Cologne European Council (June 3–4, 1999), first met in December 1999 and adopted the final draft on October 2, 2000. (*Eds.*)

28 Fischer, *Vom Staatenverbund zur Föderation* (Frankfurt, 2000).

29 Article 3 of the new Swiss constitution is noteworthy in this respect: "The Cantons are sovereign insofar as their sovereignty is not limited by the Federal Constitution and, as such, exercise all rights which are not entrusted to the federal power."

30 See the judicious proposal of the European University Institute in Florence: *Ein Basisvertrag für die Europäische Union* (Press of the European Communities, May 2000).

31 Jürgen Habermas, *Between Facts and Norms: Contributions to a Discourse Theory of Law and Democracy*, trans. William Rehg (Cambridge: Polity, 1996), ch. 9.

32 Edgar Grande, "Post-National Democracy in Europe," in Michael Greven and Louis Pauly (eds.), *Democracy beyond the State?* (Lanham, MD: Rowman and Littlefield, 2000), pp. 115–38; and "Demokratische Legitimation und europäische Integration," *Leviathan*, 24 (1996), pp. 339–60.

33 This seems more realistic than Jospin's proposal to create a further institution in the shape of a "congress" composed of delegates from national parliaments. Cf. Lars Chr. Blichner, "Interparliamentary Discourse and the Quest for Legitimacy," in Fossum and Erikson (eds.), *Democracy in the European Union*, pp. 140–63.

34 Christian Joerges and Michelle Everson, "Challenging the Bureaucratic Challenge," in Fossum and Erikson (eds.), *Democracy in the European Union*, pp. 164–88.

Chapter 8 Constitutional Democracy

1 Translated by William Rehg.

2 Habermas uses a number of terms to express the idea of the rule of law or constitutionalism (taken as equivalent for the purposes of this essay). The most literal is *Herrschaft der Gesetze*, which I always translate as "rule of law." *Rechtsstaat*, whose literal meaning is "law state," may be rendered either as "constitutional state" or "rule of law." To distinguish *Rechtsstaatlichkeit*, I translate it as "constitutionalism" or "government by law." Note, by the way, that the German word for "constitution" is *Verfassung. (Trans.)*

3 See Habermas, "On the Internal Relation between the Rule of Law and Democracy," in *The Inclusion of the Other: Studies in Political Theory*, ed. and trans. Ciaran Cronin and Pablo De Greiff (Cambridge: Polity, 1998), ch. 10.

4 Ingeborg Maus, *Zur Aufklärung der Demokratietheorie* (Frankfurt am Main: Suhrkamp, 1992).

5 Immanuel Kant, *The Conflict of the Faculties*, trans. Mary J. Gregor (New York: Abaris, 1979), p. 151 (Ak. ed. VII, p. 84).

6 *Brennan and Democracy* (Princeton: Princeton University Press, 1999).

7 Ibid., p. 59.

8 See Ronald Dworkin, *Freedom's Law: The Moral Reading of the American Constitution* (Cambridge, MA: Harvard University Press, 1996);

Robert Post, *Constitutional Domains: Democracy, Community, Management* (Cambridge, MA: Harvard University Press, 1995); Habermas's views are most fully elaborated in his *Between Facts and Norms: Contributions to a Discourse Theory of Law and Democracy*, trans. William Rehg (Cambridge: Polity, 1996). (*Trans.*)

9   Michelman, "Constitutional Authorship," in Larry Alexander (ed.), *Constitutionalism: Philosophical Foundations* (Cambridge: Cambridge University Press, 1998), pp. 64–98, here p. 90.

10 See Habermas, *Between Facts and Norms*.

11 Michelman, "Constitutional Authorship," p. 91; cf. Michelman's review of Habermas, *Between Facts and Norms*, *Journal of Philosophy*, 93 (1996), pp. 307–15; also his "Democracy and Positive Liberty," *Boston Review*, 21 (1996), pp. 3–8.

12 Michelman, "Constitutional Authorship," p. 81.

13 Habermas, *On the Pragmatics of Communication*, ed. and trans. Maeve Cooke (Cambridge, MA: MIT Press, 1998), ch. 7.

Chapter 9 John Dewey, *The Quest for Certainty*

1   John Dewey, *Die Suche nach Gewißheit* (Frankfurt am Main: Suhrkamp, 1998).

2   The translations of these Heideggerian terms are those of the older Macquarrie and Robinson translation of *Being and Time* (Oxford: Blackwell, 1980). In her more recent translation (Albany, NY: SUNY Press, 1996), Joan Stambaugh renders them, respectively, as "useful things," "handiness," and "context of relevance." (*Eds.*)

3   Dewey, *The Quest for Certainty* (New York: Milton, Balch & Co., 1929), p. 3.

Chapter 10 Richard Rorty, *Achieving Our Country*

1   German: Richard Rorty, *Stolz auf unser Land. Die amerikanische Linke und der Patriotismus*, trans. Hermann Vetter (Frankfurt am Main: Suhrkamp, 1999).

2   On Wolfgang Schäuble, see ch. 2, n. 2; on Edmund Stoiber, see ch. 3, n. 2. (*Eds.*)

3   This statement was made by the late publisher of the German weekly news magazine *Der Spiegel*, Rudolf Augstein (1923–2002). (On the public controversy surrounding the Holocaust memorial, see above pp. 45ff.) The writer alluded to in the previous sentence is the novelist Martin Walser (see above, ch. 4, n. 1). The Paulskirche occupies an important symbolic place in German history as the site of the first German constitutional convention in 1848. (*Eds.*)

4 Habermas is referring to a previous collection of his shorter political writings, *Die Normalität einer Berliner Republik. Kleine politische Schriften VIII* (Frankfurt am Main: Suhrkamp, 1995). (*Eds.*)

Chapter 11 Robert Brandom, *Making It Explicit*

1 German: Robert Brandom, *Expressive Vernunft. Begründung, Repräsentation und diskursive Festlegung*, trans. Eva Gilmer and Hermann Vetter (Frankfurt am Main: Suhrkamp, 2000).

Chapter 12 A Conversation about God and the World

1 Jürgen Habermas, *The Postnational Constellation: Political Essays*, ed. and trans. Max Pensky (Cambridge: Polity, 2001).
2 The term "Axial Age" [*Achsenzeit*] was coined by Karl Jaspers to refer to the period between 800 and 200 BCE during which, according to Jaspers, the major advances underlying all later civilization occurred concurrently and independently in China, India, the Orient, and the West. (*Eds.*)
3 Jürgen Habermas, *Knowledge and Human Interests*, trans. Jeremy J. Shapiro (Boston: Beacon Press, 1971).
4 The rabbi Isaac Luria (1534–72) was an important Jewish mystical thinker and teacher. His doctrine of *zimzum* expresses an understanding of creation as a process by which God turned back into himself or "contracted" in order to produce the void in which the imperfect world is situated. (*Eds.*)
5 I.e., the original Adam before the creation of Eve and the division of the sexes. (*Eds.*)
6 "To Seek to Salvage an Unconditional Meaning without God is a Futile Undertaking: Reflections on a Remark of Max Horkheimer," in Habermas, *Justification and Application: Remarks on Discourse Ethics*, trans. Ciaran Cronin (Cambridge: Polity, 1993), p. 146.
7 "Themes in Postmetaphysical Thinking," in Habermas, *Postmetaphysical Thinking: Philosophical Essays*, trans. William Mark Hohengarten (Cambridge: Polity, 1992), p. 51.
8 Habermas, *The Inclusion of the Other: Studies in Political Theory*, ed. and trans. Ciaran Cronin and Pablo De Greiff (Cambridge: Polity, 1999), pp. 10ff.

Index

Adenauer, Konrad, 4, 40, 84, 91
Adorno, Theodor 13, 132, 157, 159, 160, 161
Albania, 22, 23
Apel, Karl-Otto, 14, 161
Aquinas, Thomas, 154
Arendt, Hannah, 156
Arndt, Ernst-Moritz, 29
Arte Television, 103
Assheuer, Thomas, 1–15
Augstein, Rudolf, 46, 55–6

Baader, Franz von, 162
Bahr, Egon, 20
Baldwin, James, 140
Bank for International Settlements, 96
Beck, Ulrich, 28
Bell, Daniel, 5
Benjamin, Walter, 157, 159
Berlin generation, 12–13
Berlin Republic, 13, 135
Berlusconi, Silvio, 11
Between Facts and Norms, 9, 111
Bitburg, 4
Blair, Tony, 14, 83, 85
Bloch, Ernst, 157, 159

Böckenförde, Ernst-Wolfgang, 36
Böhme, Jakob, 157, 159, 162
Bohrer, Karl-Heinz, 43
Bosnia, 23, 25, 27
Brandom, Robert, 14, 129, 142–6
Brandt, Willy, 4
Brecht, Bertolt, 156
Brennan, William, 116–17
Brumlik, Mischa, 48
Buddhism, 150
Bull, Hans Peter, 33
Bush, George W, 107

Cambodia, 155
capitalism
  flexibility, 13
  global capitalism, 73–4, 83, 95, 151, 155
  global governance, 75–9
Cardiff Conference, 8
Carnap, Rudolf, 132, 143, 146
Cassirer, Ernst, 60, 61–5, 131
Charlemagne, 91
Chechnya, 27
Chicago School, 79
China, 107, 153
Chirac, Jacques, 71, 89, 106

Christianity, 149–57, 161, 166, 168
civil society, 8, 11, 88, 101–2
Cohen, Hermann, 48
Cold War, 136
colonialism, 154
communicative action, 161
cosmopolitanism, 21, 26–8, 29, 85, 88
crimes against humanity, 22
culture, 14, 53–70, 104

Dahrendorf, Ralph, 13
Darwin, Charles, 59
Davidson, Donald, 143
Dayton Accord, 23
De Gasperi, Alcide, 84, 91
Delors, Jacques, 8, 98
democracy
    classical conception, 9, 113–14
    constitutional democracy, 113–28
    deliberative democracy, 119
    and European Union, 6–7, 8, 78, 83, 98–9, 102
    global governance, 6, 75–9, 80
    and justice, 13
    party-based, 11
    and rule of law, 111, 113, 118, 127–8
Denmark, 103–4
deregulation, 6
Derrida, Jacques, 137
Dewey, John, 66, 129, 131–5, 136, 137, 144
Diepgen, Eberhard, 48
distributive justice, 12–13
Dregger, Alfred, 20, 43
Dubiel, Helmut, 47
Dummett, Michael, 143
Durkheim, Emile, 54, 56
Dworkin, Ronald, 117

Eckhart, Johannes, 157, 159
egalitarian universalism, 105–6, 150–1, 154
Emerson, Ralph Waldo, 136
empiricism, 132, 133
Enlightenment, 24, 46, 60, 161
Enzenberger, Hans Magnus, 29
Eppler, Erhard, 20
erga omnes obligations, 22
Erhart, Ludwig, 3
Erlangen school, 143
ethnic cleansing, 21–2
Euro, 6, 7, 90, 96
Eurocentrism, 154
European Central Bank, 6, 84, 98
European Union
    Charter of Fundamental Rights, 105–6
    civil society, 8, 88, 101–2
    constitution, 8, 87, 89–109
    cosmopolitanism, 85, 88
    culture, 92–4, 96, 104–6
    democracy, 6–7, 8, 78, 83, 98–9, 102
    Eurofederalism, 85, 86–7, 89, 106–9
    European Parliament, 108, 109
    Eurosceptics, 8, 73ff., 85, 86, 87, 90, 100
    ever-closer union, 90–9
    and human rights, 27
    institutions, 84, 101, 108
    languages, 103
    Market Europeans, 85–6
    Nice Treaty, 97
    post-nationalist model, 84–8
    social dimension, 8, 94, 104
    state characteristics, 99–106
    subsidiarity, 109

Fichte, Johann, 162
Fischer, Joschka, 8, 20, 24, 71, 89, 106, 107, 109

Flick affair, 35
Foucault, Michel, 36, 137, 159
France
  and European Union, 107
  Mitterrand government, 79
  Napoleonic Code, 104
  Revolution, 90, 104–5, 115,
    158
  wartime collaboration, 47
France, Anatole, 74
Frankenberg, Günter, 36
Frankfurt School, 159–61
Frege, Gottlob, 143
Fukuyama, Francis, 154
fundamentalism, 153

G-7, 167
Gehlen, Arnold, 34, 58, 60, 65–70,
    133
Genocide Convention 1948, 22
Genscher, D, 107
Germany
  anti-communism, 35
  Berlin holocaust memorial, 17,
    38–50, 55, 139, 140
  CDU political donations scandal,
    17, 31–7
  conservatives, 13, 34, 35, 138,
    139–40
  constitution, 9, 35–6
  Constitutional Court, 115–16
  culture, 14
  European integration, 91
  and European Union, 107
  and Kosovo campaign, 19–20
  Nazis, *see* Nazis
  philosophy, 131, 137, 144,
    157–64
  pietism, 153, 162
  Red-Green Coalition, 1–15, 20
  Reichstag building, 38–9
  reunification, 3, 11
  SPD, 14
  symbols and rituals, 53–70

Giesen, Bernd, 47
global governance
  democracy, 6, 75–9, 80
  and global capitalism, 73–4
  global responsibility, 167–8
  responses, 79–84
globalization, 75, 77–9, 81, 93, 95,
    149, 151, 154
Globke, Hans, 40
Goethe Institute, 14
Goldhagen, Daniel, 40, 41
Greece, Ancient, 149, 156–7,
    158
Greenpeace, 11
Grimmelshausen, Hans Jacob
    Christoph von, 29
Grünewald, Matthias, 44
Gulf War, 19, 21

Harlan, Veit, 40
Hegel, Georg, 14, 56–60, 67, 70,
    131, 137, 143, 144, 145, 146,
    157, 158, 159, 160, 162
Heidegger, Martin, 131, 132, 133,
    134, 136, 137, 146, 157, 159,
    160, 161
Heine, Heinrich, 158
Heinemann, Gustav, 4, 39
Held, David, 75
Henrich, Dieter, 158
Herzog, Roman, 39
Heuss, Theodor, 39
Hobsbawm, Eric, 93
Hofmann, Gunter, 1–15
Hölderlin, Friedrich, 158, 160
Holocaust, 40, 156, 159, 168
Holocaust Memorial, 17, 38–50,
    55, 139, 140
Horkheimer, Max, 132, 157, 163,
    164
human rights
  Anglo-American politics, 91
  and democracy, 114, 125–7
  ethnic cleansing, 21–2

EU Charter of Fundamental
Rights, 105–6
European concept, 104–5
humanitarian interventions,
21–2, 26–8, 91
legal implementation, 28, 125
and paternalism, 27–30
politics of human rights, 26–8
universalism, 155–6
Hume, David, 143
Huntington, Samuel, 154
Husserl, Edmund, 142

IMF, 96
immigration, 25
international crimes, 20
Iraq, 21, 29
Islam, 149, 154
Italy, 47

James, William, 131, 144
Jenninger, Phillip, 39
John, Otto, 40
Jospin, Lionel, 71, 93, 106, 107,
109
Judaism, 157, 162

Kant, Immanuel, 17, 20, 56, 57,
62, 114, 115, 120, 124, 143,
146, 153, 157, 158, 167
Kanther, Manfred, 32, 34, 35
Kelsen, Hans, 20
Kiep, Walter Leisler, 31
Kierkegaard, Søren, 144, 158
Knowledge and Human Interests
(Habermas), 161
Koch, Roland, 32, 34
Kohl, Helmut, 3–4, 8, 13, 31, 32,
34–6, 91
Konrád, György, 46
Korn, Salomon, 45, 48
Koselleck, Reinhart, 47, 48
Kosovo intervention
and Germany, 19–20

and paternalism, 28–30
doubtful legality, 22–4
humanitarian intervention, 21–2,
26–8, 91
NATO intervention, 17, 19–
30
Realpolitik, 24–6
Küng, Hans, 152
Kurds, 21, 27

Lafontaine, Oskar, 5, 86
Lamers, Karl, 22
languages, 8, 103–4
Lazarsfeld, Paul, 10
legal pacifism, 20, 24
liberation theology, 147, 168
Libya, 29
Lübbe, Hermann, 46, 56
Luhmann, Niklas, 9, 36, 68
Lukacs, Georg, 131
Luria, Isaac, 162
Luther, Martin, 157

Maak, Thomas, 71
Maastricht Treaty, 8
Macedonia, 22, 23
Maier, Charles, 81
Marcuse, Herbert, 13
Marx, Karl, 11, 144, 157, 158,
159
McDowell, John, 142
Mead, George Herbert, 66, 131,
134, 144
media society, 9–11
Meier, Christian, 47, 48
Melville, Gert, 51
memory
cultural memory, 53–70
Nazi era, 38–47
Mendieta, Eduardo, 147–69
Metz, Johannes Baptist, 151
Michelman, Frank, 111, 115–21,
123
Mignette, Paul, 96

Milosevic, Slobodan, 22, 23
Mitterrand, François, 79
Montenegro, 22, 23
morality, 162–3
Multilateral Agreement on
    Investment, 7
Münch, Richard, 73

Napoleonic Code, 104
nation-states
    and democracy, 75–9
    and European Union, 95–6
    EU as nation-state, 99–106
    post-nationalism, 6, 7, 11, 77,
        79–88, 83
    Westphalian concept, 24
NATO, Kosovo campaign, 17,
    19–30, 91
natural law, 124
Nazis
    and Kohl, 3, 13
    Auschwitz trials, 40
    Berlin Holocaust Memorial, 17,
        38–50, 55, 139, 140
    categories of victims, 48–50
    complicity, 40
    Holocaust, 156, 159, 168
neoliberalism, 37, 79–80, 86, 88,
    96, 154
Netherlands, 8, 47, 103–4
Nice Treaty, 97
Nietzsche, Friedrich, 36, 158, 160,
    161
North Korea, 155
Norway, 98, 104
Nuremberg trials, 22

Offe, Claus, 99

Parsons, Talcott, 54
paternalism, 28–30
Peirce, Charles Saunders, 131, 143,
    144

Perot, Ross, 11
Peru, 155
philosophical anthropology, 60ff.
philosophy
    American pragmatism, 14, 129,
        131–46
    Frankfurt School, 159–61
    German philosophy, 14, 131,
        137, 144, 157–64
    Greek, 149, 156–7, 158
Pinkard, Terry, 145
Pinochet, Augusto, 20
Pippin, Robert, 145
Platonism, 133, 134, 160
Plessner, Helmut, 60, 131
Pol Pot, 155
Post, Robert, 117
post-ideological era, 5
post-nationalism
    and welfare state, 6, 77, 83
    European Union, 84–8
    responses, 79–84
Postnational Constellation
    (Habermas), 6, 155
pragmatism, 14, 129, 131–46
Prodi, Romano, 71, 106
protectionism, 81
public sphere, 102–4, 120–1
Putnam, Hilary, 145

Quakers, 161
Quine, William, 143

race to the bottom, 6
Rambouillet negotiations, 21
Rau, Johannes, 39, 71, 106
Rawls, John, 74, 152, 167
"realism," 24–6
Red-Green Coalition, 1–15
Reformation, 152
Reichenbach, Hans, 132, 133,
    143
Reinhold, Karl, 158

religion
  and globalization, 149–56
  and morality, 162–3, 166–8
  and philosophy, 157–65
  and theology, 165
rituals, 53–70
Romans, 56, 59, 104, 157, 158
Roosevelt, F D, 28, 122, 137
Rorty, Richard, 14, 129, 133,
    136–41, 142, 146, 169
Rosenheim, Knorr von, 162
Rousseau, Jean-Jacques, 114, 115,
    124
Rühe, Volker, 20
Russia, 23, 107
Rwanda, 25

Scharping, Rudolf, 20, 24, 159
Schäuble, Wolfgang, 20, 31, 138
Scheler, Max, 60, 61, 131, 132,
    133
Schelling, Friedrich, 158, 159, 162
Schmidt, Helmut, 3, 25, 25, 96
Schmitt, Carl, 4, 24, 35
Scholem, Gershom, 49, 162
Schröder, Gerhard, 6–7, 13, 14,
    38–9, 71, 85, 86, 106, 140
Schumann, Robert, 84, 91
Sellars, Wilfred, 144
Sennett, Richard, 12
Serbia, 21–2, 23, 27, 28, 29
Siedentop, Larry, 89
Somalia, 25
South Africa, 47
Spain, 47
Srebenica, 27
Stoiber, Edmund, 34, 138
Strauss, Botho, 13, 43
Streeck, Wolfgang, 78, 80
Stroeble, Hans-Christian, 20
Suhr, Martin, 131
Sweden, 47, 104
Switzerland, 98

symbolic forms, 62–5
symbols, 53–70

television, 9–10, 103, 139
Telò, Mario, 96
Thatcher, Margaret, 83
Therborm, Göran, 94
Third Way, 37, 74, 79, 81–4, 85,
    86
Tibet, 27
Tietmeyer, Hans, 85
Tokyo trials, 22
Toledo, 149
Trotskysm, 137

Uexküll, Johannes von, 61
Ulrich, Peter, 71
unemployment, 5, 11
United Kingdom, 91, 107
United Nations
  and crimes against humanity,
    22
  and European Union, 107
  and Gulf War, 21
  and human rights, 26, 28
  and Iraq, 21
  and Kosovo, 29, 91
  and Srebenica, 27
  cosmopolitanism, 29
  creation, 21, 26
United States
  and human rights, 27, 30, 91
  and Kosovo, 91
  and WTO, 81
  Bush administration, 107
  colonial history, 47
  constitutional history, 122
  cultural Left, 136–41
  culture, 14
  democratic process, 11
  Founding Fathers, 90
  philosophical pragmatism, 14,
    129, 131–46

United States (*cont'd*)
  superpower, 27–8
  Supreme Court, 115–16
  Vietnam War, 27, 136, 137
  Vietnam War Memorial, 47
Universal Declaration of Human
    Rights, 26
universalism
  egalitarian universalism, 105–6,
    150–1, 154
  human rights, 155–6
  religions, 150–1, 153

Verdun, 4
Vico, Giambattista, 67
Vietnam War, 27, 47, 136, 137

Waigel, Theo, 6
Walser, Martin, 38, 46, 56
Warburg Circle, 62
Weber, Max, 54, 90, 150
Weiss, Peter, 40
welfare state, 6, 11, 77, 83, 98
Westphalia, Peace of (1648), 24
Weyrauch, Horst, 35
Whitman, Walt, 136, 137
Wilson, Woodrow, 28
Wittgenstein, Ludwig, 131, 133,
    143, 146, 159, 161
World Bank, 96
WTO, 81, 93

Zizek, Slavoj, 28